Vanya

MYRNA GRANT

Creation House
Carol Stream, Illinois

© 1974 by Creation House. All rights reserved.
Published by Creation House,
396 E. St. Charles Rd., Carol Stream, Illinois 60187
In Canada: Beacon Distributing Ltd.,
104 Consumers Drive, Whitby, Ontario L1N 5T3.

All biblical quotations reprinted with permission
from the New American Standard Bible
© 1971 by the Lockman Foundation.

First printing, March 1974
Second printing, June 1974
Third printing, April 1975

New Leaf Library Edition
First Printing, November 1975
Second Printing, August 1976
Third Printing, April 1978
Fourth Printing, January, 1980
"Fifth printing January 1981"

International Standard Book Number 0-88419-009-9
Library of Congress Catalog Card Number 73-89729

In keeping silent about evil, in burying it deep within us, so that it appears nowhere on the surface, we are implanting it, and it will rise up a thousandfold in the future.

Alexander Solzhenitsyn
The Gulag Archipelago

Contents

Foreword   7

Preface   11

Part One   The Story   15

Part Two   The Documents   153

  Transcript of Vanya's taped account   154

  Entries from Vanya's notebook   168

  Excerpts from Vanya's last letters   170

  The funeral document   177

  The open letter from Vanya's church   182

  The Moiseyevs' formal protest to the world   185

  The Moiseyevs' appeal to their church leadership   190

  The underground news bulletin   192

  Press "explanations" of Ivan's death   194

  Condolences to the Moiseyevs   204

Ivan Moiseyev at the time he was drafted (November 1970).

Ivan in uniform (May 1972).

Foreword

On July 16, 1972, a young man, a soldier, died in the Crimea. He was a church member, and his death was a violent one. Details of how it happened and why are told in this moving book. Documentary evidence at the Centre for the Study of Religion and Communism confirms the facts related in this book.

Vanya's death was an event out of the ordinary, and it turned the attention of thousands, probably millions of people all over the world, to the Soviet Union and its religious policy. The murder of this young Baptist was not an everyday occurrence. The community of churches to which he belonged brackets it together with the murder of Nikolai Khmara in a Siberian prison, which took place as long ago as 1964. Young Baptists in the USSR compose poems about these two martyrs and read them in meetings to encourage the believers. But although the death of Vanya Moiseyev was untypical, it highlighted a situation which demands the concern of Christians and, indeed, all people of good will everywhere.

The fact is that Soviet hostility toward religion has not changed since the Bolshevik revolution. Actual tactics have swung between violent and illegal persecution and a more subtle propaganda approach. But at no time has the Soviet leadership abandoned its declared aim of rooting out all religious survivals.

This militantly atheistic policy has affected all churches in the Soviet Union. In the early years after 1917 it was the ancient, established Orthodox church which suffered the full force of the atheist onslaught, while the Baptists and other denominations enjoyed a relative freedom—which they used to the full. But it was not long, as Stalin took the reins of power more and more firmly into his own hands, until all the churches felt the cold wind.

During the terror of the 1930s, thousands of Christians and others suffered and died in Stalin's purges. But the Second World War changed the situation abruptly. The government found itself in need of maximum support from the people as the country suffered heavier and heavier losses. Appeal was made to Russian patriotism, and the churches were encouraged to rally their members to the national cause. Concessions were made in private interviews between Stalin and certain church leaders, and these led to a relaxation of pressure and, in turn, to a religious renaissance that probably surprised the authorities.

But the new policy did not last long. As the immediate crisis passed, so old patterns of repression returned. Then came Khrushchev. Despite his popular image as a "liberalizer," Khrushchev in fact unleashed a vicious campaign against religion that lasted from 1959 until his fall from power in 1964. It is reckoned that half the Orthodox churches in the country were closed. The Baptists also suffered from the new repression.

One aspect of this was the introduction of some new statutes which, although presented by the Baptist leadership to the churches, were clearly the result of state pressure.

8

This unhappy situation caused a sharp reaction among Baptist believers throughout the country. An action group was set up to agitate for a congress to set things right. This aim was not achieved, and in 1965 the split in Baptist ranks became final.

The reforming group which split away in 1965 exists to this day in a technically illegal condition. It calls itself the Council of Churches of Evangelical Christians/Baptists, and it was to this movement that Vanya Moiseyev belonged. The leaders of this group call for an uncompromising loyalty to Christ, for continual spiritual renewal, for evangelism. They also call for justice toward Soviet believers; they appeal to the Soviet Constitution and to the original decrees of Lenin. They can thus be seen within the context of the wider Soviet human rights movement, to which they have contributed much. Indeed they may be said to have blazed the trail for much that was to follow: human rights activity in the USSR which has hit the headlines in recent years. It was the Baptists first who, in a highly organized fashion, produced unofficial documents, lists, and even regular journals telling about their life and problems. The Baptists are the only group in the Soviet Union to have produced regular lists of their members in prison, giving unbelievably detailed information, including addresses of hundreds of labor camps. These data have been of incalculable value to researchers on modern Soviet society. The Baptists are the only dissenting group in the Soviet Union to operate a clandestine printing press. Called "The Christian," it has been in operation at least since 1971 and probably earlier.

This is the background against which the murder of Vanya Moiseyev must be seen. It was a brutal act, revealing the fear and anger of a small number of men in authority. And yet at the same time it was the manifestation of a hostility that is constant and which threatens at any time to erupt in such violence. It is to be hoped that antireligious campaigns like those under Stalin and Khrushchev will not recur. One factor to prevent their recurrence would certainly be the continuing concern and positive action of all those who read this book and who care about the fate of Soviet Christians today.

MICHAEL BOURDEAUX
Director, Centre for the Study
of Religion and Communism

Chislehurst, Kent, England

Preface

Holiday crowds were pouring out of the circus, tourists from all over the Soviet Union and eastern Europe, children with dazzled eyes, students and local families out for a treat. The fountains of the circus plaza sprayed cooling patterns in the south Russian heat. But through the crowd, a terrified man was walking quickly, his eyes searching for the American friends he had promised to meet.

The night before I had sat in the single "prayer house" serving his city of a million people, listening to him preach a radiant sermon on the power of God. He had cited David Livingstone and Dostoevsky as examples for the congregation—men who had ventured all for their faith.

Now, less than twenty-four hours later, he was being closely trailed by the KGB, and he knew it. His mind churned in a torment of anxiety for what he might bring upon his family, his church, his American friends—all because of a clandestine agreement after the church service to meet the next day and talk.

On the plaza, in those moments of fear, I was plunged with him into the suffering subculture of the Soviet Christian.

11

I too felt panic. The pastor's words were frantic: "I can't talk; I'm being followed—God bless you—good-by." Instantly he fled into the crowds. Why? Why should the secret police be immediately concerned that two American Christians and a Russian pastor should privately talk?

It was at this point that I knew Ivan's book had to be written. In a more intensified form, his is the story of all believers in the Soviet Union—gentle, humble citizens whose lives are a kaleidoscope of fear, uncertainty, caution, sacrifice, incredible courage, endurance, and triumph.

It was sometimes difficult inside Russia to ask about Ivan, because the KGB was conducting an aggressive campaign to find and destroy the documents which appear in this book and to threaten and arrest believers who passed on the story. But in spite of the danger, believers were eager to talk. Often tears sprang to the eyes of men as well as women as they said, "*Verno, Verno.*" ("It is true. It is true.") Nowhere in any city did I ever ask about Ivan and find his story not known and verified.

A young woman chemical engineer from Omsk in Siberia told me of a compulsory political meeting called in her factory to denounce the "false rumors" of Ivan's death and to provide the official statement.

In the Georgian republic I shared a park bench with a middle-aged mother whose eyes were red from weeping. I had arranged earlier to meet her, and she was keeping the appointment in spite of her great distress. The night before, while she was at the prayer house, the secret police had searched her home. They were looking for Moiseyev documents but had found none. (She had passed some along only the day before.) Instead, her few religious papers and bits of Scripture had been taken. Her voice was tightly controlled as she told her story, at the end breaking down into weeping and repeating the words, "It's terrible. It's terrible."

In western Europe more information came from Ivan's former youth pastor from Moldavia. Because of having close relatives in Germany, his family had been permitted to emigrate. Also present was a believer from Ivan's church who had attended his funeral. All of them wanted to talk about Ivan's fervent faith and to give what help they could for this book. Each one could have told his own story of personal suffering if he had wished.

The Russian author Alexander Solzhenitsyn continues to focus world attention on the suppression of basic human rights within the USSR. He is one of several famous spokesmen for the present dissident movement in the Soviet Union, an action group of intellectuals who plead eloquently for freedom of thought and expression and denounce the Soviet system of police terror. As I write, the Soviet government has exiled him following the Paris publication of his explosive book *The Gulag Archipelago*.

What is not well-known in the free world is that there is another heroic protest movement in the Soviet Union. It has risen from the ranks of the repressed and suffering evangelical churches all over the USSR. Some local churches protest individually. Since 1964 there has been an organization in Moscow called poignantly "The Council of Prisoners' Relatives." This group appeals for religious freedom and resolutely protests the discrimination, persecution, arrests, and sometimes killings of Christian believers in the USSR.

In contrast to Solzhenitsyn, the council has no protection in the form of international publicity. Its leaders have been consistently arrested or exiled. New leaders of the same courageous caliber step into the vacant places and its activities continue.

It was to this council that the parents of Ivan Vasilievich* Moiseyev appealed for help. Through its efforts his story was successfully brought out to the West. Men, women, and young people within this group risked their freedom and their lives to protest Ivan's death.

People of good will the world over are repelled by the denial of basic human rights in a totalitarian society. But that is not enough. There must be a mobilization of revulsion, a ground swell, an outcry on all levels of free society on behalf of these powerless people who are the subjects of repression.

Vanya's story I have written down, remembering the Voice that spoke to John in Patmos saying, "What thou seest, write in a book." That same Voice also said, "Be ye doers . . . and not hearers only."

---

*For readers unfamiliar with Russian nomenclature: middle names are formed from the father's first name plus a masculine or feminine ending (-*vich* or -*ova*). Thus *Ivan Vasilievich* means *Ivan, son of Vasiliy* (which is not unlike the biblical format, e.g., David the son of Jesse).

Though it may sound awkward to North Americans, Russians generally call each other by both the first and middle names.

Part One
The Story

1

He who weeps from the heart can provoke even the blind to tears.*

*The chapter epigraphs throughout the book are traditional Russian proverbs.

Joanna Constantinova didn't want it to be time for the coffin to arrive. Ever since the telegram had come from the army on the seventeenth, she had dreaded this moment above all others. She slowly turned her swollen eyes to the place in the crowded parlor where her husband, Vasiliy Trofimovich, was standing. A group of brothers from the prayer house stood with him, their faces profoundly grave. Only her husband's face was hidden, his head bent sharply toward the painted floor.

But the moment was here. The pickup truck bearing Vanya's coffin from the train station was grinding to a stop in the rutted road outside. Through the lace curtains, motionless in the July heat, Joanna could see the military escort vehicle pulling up behind the truck. Three men in the gray dress uniforms of the Soviet army stood stiffly beside their Pobeda as the coffin was carefully pushed from the truck bed and eased onto the shoulders of the sweating pallbearers. Her son, Semyon, directed them through the wooden gate and toward the house.

At the sight of the soldiers, Joanna's terrible fear of what she might do left her. There would be no crying out, no fainting at the sight of her dead son. If there were to be difficulties, she would need all the will she had. Her eyes met her husband's. He too was ready. A holy strength seemed upon him.

The two officers and a young private entered the room awkwardly, bending their heads to pass beneath the low door frame, uncomfortably aware that they were unwelcome in the suddenly charged atmosphere of the congested parlor. The village people pulled away from them, making a small path through the crowd that ended before the person of Vasiliy Trofimovich.

The coffin advanced, held aloft by four of the young people

18

who had been Vanya's friends. Joanna was shocked at its huge size and the expensive gleam of the metal. Her husband swayed slightly as the young men lowered it onto the table she had made ready. Most of the women in the room wore their dark babushkas pulled low over their foreheads. A few now began to weep, hiding their faces behind white hankerchiefs so that their heads were completely covered with cloth.

For the first time Joanna noticed that the coffin was welded shut and sealed with several insignias of the Soviet army. The senior officer, Captain Platonov of Special Affairs, cleared his throat nervously, bowing slightly to the parents. "On behalf of our Lieutenant Colonel V. Malsin and the officers and men of Unit 61968T, I extend to the parents and relatives and comrades of Private Ivan* Vasilievich Moiseyev our condolences on the tragic death of this young Soviet soldier." His eyes moved uneasily from face to face about the room, each pair of eyes returning his gaze.

Under her shawl Joanna fingered the letters Ivan had sent the last few days before his death. As if to hold back part of her son from the captain, she pressed the thin letters to herself, shielding them with the flat of her hand from Platonov's lies. She had arranged them in a small packet according to the postmarks smeared in red ink over the red stamps: June 15, 1972; June 30, 1972; July 9, 1972; July 14, 1972; July 15, 1972. She felt the dates crying out against her hand, protesting the hypocrisy before the casket. Condolences! Her eyes burned.

"Of course we shall require that my son's coffin be opened." Vasiliy Trofimovich's voice was steady.

"But that is not necessary!" Platonov spoke more sharply than he intended, his tone jerking up some of the bowed heads at the back of the sweltering room. "Your son's body has already been identified in Kerch by yourself and your son, Semyon Vasilievich." He pressed a folded handkerchief to his forehead before continuing in a softer voice. "Such a terrible

---

*The Russian pronunciation is e-*von*. Hence, the familiar nickname *Vanya*.

accident has been a great shock to you and your wife. You must spare yourselves further distress." His words became almost a whisper. "Death by drowning can be . . . very disfiguring."

With her free hand, Joanna pushed to her husband's side. "Comrade Officer—?"

"Platonov."

"Platonov. As Ivan's mother I insist that the coffin be opened. I wish to see my son. And we desire him to be buried in civilian clothes. That is our right."

A crowbar was passed through the crowd and handed to Vasiliy. Platonov bent in a whispered conversation with his two companions. After a moment, Vasiliy fitted the crowbar's tip into the space under the top of the coffin. The special officer, with a motion of his hand, detained him. "I regret, Comrade Moiseyev, that another duty calls us away immediately. What you are determined to do is very foolish." With a glance at Semyon standing beside the father, the three men made their way through the crowd and disappeared.

Again Vasiliy raised the crowbar to the top of the casket and pushed down. At the same instant that the coffin creaked, so many things occurred at once that Joanna stood gaping, unable to make out what was happening. Like a madman, Semyon hurled himself onto the coffin, flinging his arms over the top, his voice a strangled protest. "Papa! No! Papa! Don't open it!"

The crowbar crashed to the floor. Vasiliy tried to push his eldest son out of the way. People were crowding forward to see what was causing the disturbance. "What's going on?"— "Semyon is fighting his father."—"Not fighting. He won't let him open the coffin."—"Who's fighting? I can't see." —"What a shameful thing! His own brother."

Two of the pastors, their thin shirts wet under heavy black suits, moved quickly toward Semyon, each to pull an arm and successfully drag him away from the coffin. A few women in the back of the room began praying aloud, their frightened petitions rising and falling in a rapid torrent of emotion and tears. Semyon grappled desperately against the restraint of the pastors, lurching back toward the coffin, his voice muffled. "Papa! Papa! Momma! Please! Let Vanya be! Don't open the coffin."

Joanna stared at her son. In the midst of the confusion, a great weariness came upon her. Long ago she had been proud of Semyon's boyish ambitions, his dreams to advance beyond the backbreaking labor of the collective, to make a place for himself in one of the administrative committees of the farm. He had been a hard worker, and when one day he had come home from school wearing the red scarf of the Young Pioneers,* the family's disapproval could not persuade him to take it off. He had become the Moiseyev to be reckoned with, full of self-assurance, confident of his future. Now, seeing the frenzy of fear that reduced Semyon to begging like a terrified child, she looked away. All the wonderful advantages of the Komsomol had brought him to this: orders from the party to help them hide his own brother's body.

The pastors were pushing Semyon through the crowd, outside into the tiny garden of cabbages and roses that lay untended. There was a renewed scuffle at the door; then it was quietly shut. Vasiliy leaned on the crowbar, and the slight, splintering sound of pressure drew the attention of the villagers to the coffin, now lit by the early afternoon sun. Fearfully, the top was raised.

The pastors filed forward and glanced hesitantly at the body. Panic twisted wildly inside Joanna as she saw the look of horror that passed over their faces. One of the oldest, Fyodor Gorektoi, leaned his white head against the coffin, his eyes averted. Tears poured down his weathered face. In fear,

---

*Virtually all Russian children belong to the Young Pioneers, the Communist Party organization for ages 9-14. It provides all their camping, athletic, musical and cultural training.

The Komsomol, for ages 15-28, continues the activities of the Young Pioneers but with intensive indoctrination; members must be atheists. The Komsomol is the introduction to the full party membership.

Joanna clutched the hand of the sister beside her. An arm went around her and led her slowly to the coffin. Joanna heard her husband sobbing. The sound seemed far away. Her trembling body moved toward the body of her son, but everything within her seemed to flee back, out of herself, out of the room, away from the thing she could not bear to see.

She forced her eyes to look into the casket and gazed in bewilderment at the body inside. It wasn't Vanya! She continued to stare, troubled that she felt no surge of relief. It was some older soldier, heavy-jowled, his face bruised badly on both sides, as if from a desperate fight. The mouth was swollen, somehow broken, and the forehead and sides of the head were blackened and oddly lumped. His dark hair was brushed away from his face in some way like Vanya's. Her heart lurched. Someone close by moaned terribly. Suddenly her eyes blurred with tears. It was her Vanya. She slumped and began again to weep.

2

Hope in the Lord,
but exert yourself.

Ivan was filled with praise as he strode across the blackened vineyards under the icy November sky. The hymns of the evening turned in his mind and he half-sung, half-spoke his thoughts to God.

"Thank You for the young people, for the farewell meeting, for the bread and grapes and honey. For the fresh grape juice from our own Moldavian fields, for Boris and Vladimir and Luba and Yakov and Victor and Svetlana. Praise to You, Lord for Your Word, for the preaching of Stefan and Sasha. For the birthday of Elena Kuzminichna that permitted us to have a meeting."

His mother, gazing from the tiny frosted window of her kitchen, followed his moonlit progress over the fields. "What's to become of him in the army, I wonder?" She spoke more to herself than to her husband, who was cleaning his boots by the gas heater.

He dropped a boot heavily to the floor and straightened his back. "Thus far the Lord has helped us," he quoted from the Old Testament. Vasiliy was a man who hoped to live quietly and avoid trouble when he could. "We've had our times, all right." His wife nodded without turning her head from the window. He was thinking about the Stalin years. Vasiliy had once heard a tourist in the city say twenty million Russians had been killed in those times.

It couldn't have been that many, she knew. Joanna sighed. It wasn't like her to be troubled. Vasiliy watched her thoughtfully as she moved toward the brick stove to add a piece of wood. "He's only eighteen. Only a believer two years. It's going to be hard for him." Her babushka had slipped back on her head like a young girl's. She reached for the box of tea. "He'll be wanting a hot drink."

Her voice was low but she spoke without whispering. It was a particularly Russian art, Vasiliy thought, this manner of quiet speech. Even in families but certainly in public places and at work, one spoke softly and without emphasis. Moldavians like them had had to learn it.

The curtains lifted in alarm as Ivan opened the door and slipped in, pulling gloves off his reddened fingers.

Joanna could read in his smile what a wonderful evening it had been. "Many young people?" She lifted the kettle onto the stove.

"Everybody. Stefan and Sasha spoke."

"Oh, Stefan and Sasha spoke!" Semyon ducked out of the bedroom where the younger children were sleeping on their couches and cots. He enjoyed making his parents a little uneasy. They didn't like him to hear conversations about the believers. The fact that they pretended not to care amused him.

"Hello, Vanya. Home from your secret meeting?"

"It was Elena Kuzminichna's birthday, Semyon. You ought to have come."

"And the fact that this is your last night before leaving for two years in the army had nothing to do with the meeting. I'm sure no one paid any attention."

"You're welcome to tea, Semyon." Joanna set out the glasses with some irritation. Was Semyon going to argue on Vanya's last night?

"At least Stefan spoke! That must have taken the eyes of the girls off of one Ivan Vasilievich for some moments!" Semyon laughed as a blush deepened on Ivan's face.

Joanna smiled. "He'll make a good-looking soldier." How could Semyon understand about the preaching of the Word?

"He made a good-looking taxi driver. I don't know what all your customers will do tomorrow when you're gone! I can just hear all the old babushkas crying on the way to the clinic. 'Where is young Vanya?' "

"They'd soon forget about me, if you would be kind to them."

25

Semyon choked on the word. *"Kindness!* That is not a Bolshevik word. Kindness and love! Love is a biological reaction. Everybody knows that." His eye caught his mother's flowered cardboard motto on the kitchen wall. "God is love? How can a God who is supposedly spirit have biological reactions?"

"Your love for Momma is biological?" Ivan set his empty tea glass on the table thoughtfully.

"Of course. There is a dependence tie because she is my parent. Papa too."

"And when you marry? Will you not love your wife?"

"That is more biological than ever!" Semyon smiled in a small triumph. "At first, it will be sexual attraction; then, I hope, friendship based on mutual respect."

Joanna shook the fire so vigorously that red embers fell into the smoking ash box. Her husband began cleaning his second boot.

Ivan drew his chair closer to his brother. "And Moldavia? What of the love you feel for Moldavia? What is that?"

Semyon tipped his chair back in a position of supreme thought, bringing it down upon the floor with a decisive bang. "I am trying to tell you that you won't find kindess and love in the Red army. Life there is no joke. It's nothing to me if you won't listen. You can sit there and smile if you like. But you won't smile after tomorrow."

Ivan's look of confidence included his parents. "Of course I'll smile, Semyon. It is not the government that insists I join the army for my time of service. It is the Lord who puts me there. And will He now leave me? I don't think so!"

Semyon attempted a shrug. "There's no point in discussing it. You're determined to have a hard time. So good-night!" He picked up the blanket and pillow being warmed on the chair by the gas heater and made for the small porch on which he slept. At the door he turned. "It's not only that you'll make the usual happy fool of yourself talking about God and praying all the time. I am telling you, such activities are not allowed. It is not

26

my fault if you won't listen to me." The springs of his cot creaked repeatedly as he flung himself down and began pulling off his boots.

Vasiliy Trofimovich broke the uneasy silence. His voice was so low Joanna stopped shaking the fire to hear him. "You have to do what God tells you, son. We know that. If what Semyon says is true . . . ." His voice trailed off helplessly. He stared for a moment at the glowing embers in the ash box. "I wish there were some way I could help you." His eyes searched his son's face lovingly. "Your mother and I, all the family, all the brethren will continue in prayer for you. You know that."

Joanna had left her crouched position by the stove and, putting the ashes to one side, sat down again beside her husband, her right hand reaching for a basket of handwork. A draught from the window blew the thin drapes hanging in the entranceway into the room as if they too were trying to hear the conversation between father and son.

There was a sureness about Vanya that didn't belong to his eighteen years. She had seen it in the brothers who returned from terms in labor camps. They had faced the worst and found it to be endurable. It was as if the camp were still within them, and they moved in a way different from other men. There was a common saying that the only place to be free is in prison, because everything has already been lost. Yet Vanya had this freedom.

It was as if he had never learned to be cautious, to glance behind him before speaking, to take measure of who was nearby. Even in the registered prayer houses, believers had many fears. A police informer might observe a believer talking too long to a visitor. A pastor might make too many visits to homes. He might preach too enthusiastically or fail to report any irregularity in his congregation. Among unregistered congregations such as theirs discretion was even more a way of life. But not for Vanya.

With a glance at Semyon's room that she could not resist, Joanna leaned out of the light that fell on her sewing to hear her son's voice. Even in the shadow she could see the relaxed confidence in his face.

"Once I had a dream," he was saying softly. "I was standing watch with an angel on a large rock. A great storm came up. I was frightened and saw a ship floundering in the high seas. People were drowning and the angel told me to jump into the sea and save them. I remember I was in the water and somehow dragged many people to shore. The waves roared, and when I pulled the last person out, I fell down without strength. But the angel picked me up and put me back on the rock, and there I stood guard again."

Joanna wished she knew what her husband was thinking. What could be made of Vanya's strange stories? But Vasiliy Trofimovich sat in silence, his head toward his son as if he were still speaking. Vanya continued.

"The Lord has told me to speak for Him wherever I am and not to be silent. This confirms what our pastors say when they preach that we must witness to God's love and not be fearful about consequences. Stefan spoke of this tonight—that we are all to preach the gospel wherever we are: in school, in our work, wherever, following the examples of the prophets and apostles."

Vasiliy hesitated before he spoke. At last he turned, smiling slightly to his son. He leaned toward him, and after a long embrace replied, "So you must obey God, Vanya. So we will pray."

The night was long for Vasiliy Trofimovich. While all the children slept, Ivan with his already packed suitcase beside the couch that was his bed, Vasiliy knelt near the stove in a blanket, striving in prayer for his son.

3

*No threshold
without God.*

It was almost two in the morning and Ivan's head was swimming with sleep. It was colder in Odessa than it had been in Moldavia. The snow was not yet deep, but its surface was frozen and slippery as the draftees jumped down from the oppressive warmth of the army trucks that had brought them from the train station. Now, as they half-slid, half-ran to keep up with an escort car that directed them to a cluster of buildings ahead in the darkness, Ivan tried to make sense out of the confusion of voices calling from different places in the darkness.

"Over here—quickly!" "Convoy's an hour late. We've been waiting out here one hour." "Stand at attention! What's the matter with all you stragglers? Quickly now!" "How are they going to be assigned to beds at this hour, I'd like to know? There's a regulation that all new arrivals must be here before ten P.M." "What do you want to do, then? Stand them in the cold all night?" "Who's to give the welcome?" "Where's Karetko?" "Someone run for Karetko. They're here."

A dim figure in a greatcoat and scarf wrapped almost to the tip of his officer's hat clumsily mounted a few steps of the building before which the freezing group had come to a halt. He addressed them in muffled shouts. Because of the lateness of the hour, he barked, greetings would be brief and the men would be dismissed to their barracks for the night. The barracks were the large buildings facing directly onto the square in which they were standing. As they could see in the floodlights, the buildings were five stories high. Each floor of each building consisted of six dormitories, each one accommodating thirty-two soldiers, so there would be 192 men to a floor. The men had received coupons on the train designating the number of their barrack, their floor, and their room. Officers were present who would direct new soldiers to their bunks.

The officer paused suddenly to clear his throat, pull his scarf out of the way, and spit emphatically into the snow.

They would be awakened at six A.M. by a bugle call. They would have five minutes to get up and dressed and make their beds. At that time they would receive further instructions. Dismissed. The muffled figure wheeled into the open door behind him.

Immediately a frenzied kaleidoscope of activity began. Officers sprang to life—pushing, shouting, scattering small groups of men in different directions. Inside the barracks the weary draftees pushed through the rows of bunks in the glare of bare light bulbs in the ceiling. In a search hurried by the cries of officers, they looked for numbers that corresponded to the rumpled blue coupons they held in their hands, like so many late theatergoers looking for their seats after the first-act curtain.

Accents strange to Ivan filled the rooms—Lithuanians making themselves understood in broken Russian, Byelorussians, the famous Moscow accent blending with the slower, softer speech of the North—and at every turn, the blur of fatigue that churned the whole mosaic of bunks, arms, legs, laughter, and cursing into a tumble of unreality.

By morning a light snow was falling. Tiny flakes fell on his lashes and the rim of his bugle as Boris Yakovlevich Frolov raised his instrument for reveille. Grimly he pointed it at the windows on the third floors of the barracks where he knew the new recruits had been taken during the night. Never too soon to discover the rigors of army life! Taking a blast of cold air into his lungs, he blew.

Only too well he could imagine the scene in those rooms: the apprehensive rush to get dressed, not to be left behind, not to be singled out as slow or stupid. The strangeness of their new uniforms would begin now, and the mutual sizing-up, and the cold walk to the mess hall for a breakfast of fish and tea. The first day of running from drill to class to orientation to meals to gymnastics was upon them. He blew the bugle again in an opposite direction. For him, only eleven months left. That was something to be thankful for. Already the men in his own unit were hurrying out of the barracks stripped to the waist for running. They would cover their course of fifteen kilometers in the hour before breakfast.

Boris Yakovlevich lowered his bugle and marched the goose step to his barracks. Perhaps today at target practice he would save a bullet for himself. It was an idea that haunted him.

The important thing, Ivan was thinking as he made his way to the dining hall, *is to find a place to pray.* Already the crowds of soldiers, the noise in the barracks, the difficulty in being alone pressed upon him. Even the bare poplar trees he passed huddled together in thickets as if it would be suspect to grow in solitude.

The smoky smell of sturgeon hung over the vast mess hall as Ivan joined a long line for the mugs of tea that steamed invitingly in the cold. At home at this hour, he would be praying. Prayer times were easy to arrange at home, even in the busy days when he was taking his chauffeur's training at the institute. There were hours in which he could pray before his train left for the city. In the winter on a morning like this, two of the younger children would be bedded on top of the kitchen stove, hunched together for warmth. It had been pleasant to pray beside them as they slept, their regular breathing undisturbed by the soft rising and falling of his voice.

Perhaps after the meal he could look for a quiet place. The plates of fish were empty now, but every one of the thirty soldiers at the table was still hungry, passing the plates of dark bread up and down until they too were bare. An orderly moved among the rows of tables with a huge kettle of tea, slopping out extras of the tepid drink into uplifted metal cups.

A feeling of loneliness tightened Ivan's throat. It was as he expected, of course, but perhaps he had underestimated the enormity of the task ahead of him. Each person seemed caught up in a microcosm of his own: choking down the last dregs of tea, wiping up a plate with a crumpled bit of bread, climbing over the bench deftly balancing plate and cup, hurrying to the door, stopping to chat with a friend made on the train. Lines of soldiers pressed in at the entrance as others pushed through them into the icy November dawn. "Confess Me before men and I will acknowledge you before the angels of God." There was no questioning that Voice that had spoken so many times in his spirit. Ivan put his fork and spoon in the mug on his plate and lifted himself back over the bench, moving with the others toward the door. The first thing to do was to find a place to pray.

Staff Sergeant Strelkov had a long smooth face with hollow cheeks he sucked in when irritated. For two weeks he had been trying to get the new unit in shape; two weeks of the invariable questions, disorder, and interruptions he detested. A clump of icy mud clung to his boot and he kicked it off impatiently. This new lot was a poor bunch. His eyes, narrowed in the cold, shifted to the place in the shivering formation where a man was missing. Movement on the near edge of the drill grounds caught his eye. He watched impassively as the straggler approached in a desperate run. It was Moiseyev.

Gasping for breath, he took his place in the line. Not a man moved so much as a sideway glance. Strelkov was slightly gratified. Perhaps a lesson could be made of this.

"Give your reason for being late, Comrade Private Moiseyev." Strelkov's disciplined bearing was mute witness to the fact that he himself had never once been late.

Ivan's bare chest was heaving from the long run across the field. Uneasily he viewed the ramrod form of the sergeant as he steadied his breathing. A tension slowly built in the forma-

33

tion as Strelkov's question awaited an answer.

"I am sorry, sir. I was praying, sir."

Strelkov stared. There was no hint of the buffoon in Moiseyev's grave expression. Someone in the line coughed suddenly. Strelkov glared at the motionless men. Did they think he didn't know they were suffocating with laughter?

Strelkov had been in the army long enough to know how to handle irregularities. "You will drill with the unit, Moiseyev. When we have completed the exercises, you will report to me." He stepped back to address the formation, his order scattering the men to different sections of the field to begin their drills. In an instant the grounds were alive with bodies leaping, jogging, arms flashing in exercise formations.

Ivan longed to throw himself into performing the calisthenics, to purge himself of the shame of being late and of abusing the wonderful gift the Lord had given him. How easy it had been to rejoice at finding an unused office for a prayer room. The old babushka sweeping the floor had assured him the room was not in use until ten in the morning. She herself unlocked the door at five when she came to clean. Praise had rolled over Ivan every morning since, as the stillness of the place settled in on his soul. There was a leather chair so that he could kneel on the floor, leaning his elbows on the seat, shielded by its generous back from a cracked window.

But to forget the time! To be late for drill. With a renewed pang of embarrassment he heard Strelkov calling him again.

The sergeant's atheism was third-generation. His grandfather had been one of the earliest Bolsheviks, a midshipman on the battleship *Aurora* who had fought in the streets of Leningrad during the Revolution. During the Great Patriotic War his father had been an officer in the seige of Leningrad and had died of wounds and hunger in the last days of the seige. His Communist Party card had been in his pocket when he died. Strelkov carried his father's card next to his own in his wallet.

He was disturbed by the presence of what he called "bour-

34

geois remnants" in the army. He rubbed his gloves together and began walking, indicating with a jerk of his head that Ivan was to follow. "What's this about praying, Moiseyev? You weren't joking?"

"No, sir."

"Then what's the matter with you?"

"Nothing, sir. I feel fine."

"Orthodox? Are you a churchman?" Strelkov tried to think if today was a religious day for the Orthodox. Every now and then there would be incidents on religious days.

"No, sir. Baptist."

That was worse. Baptists* were unpredictible and stubborn. In the Komsomol, Strelkov had conducted antireligious seminars in rural communities. The Baptists attended, but they frequently gave such lengthy answers to religious questions that it was difficult to best them.

"That won't do here, Moiseyev. Praying. Religion. Not in the Red army. It is unfortunate to find religious survivals anywhere in Soviet life but especially so in a young man training in the army of the Union of Soviet Socialist Republics. It is certain that you will have to change your ideas."

Ivan continued walking silently with the officer, wondering if an answer was expected of him.

"I am sure after you make some friends, begin to enjoy army life a little more, you will see the childishness of your religious ideas. It was only after Russia threw off the shackles of the czar and the church that she was able to become strong. It is the same for a man." In spite of his greatcoat, Strelkov was getting chilled. He ought to be inside at his desk. He glanced at Ivan. His skin was bright with the cold.

---

*In the USSR, the word *Baptist* is a general term meaning *Protestant,* as contrasted with *churchman,* which refers to a member of the Russian Orthodox Church. There are two groups of Protestants: the government-registered All-Union Council of Evangelical Christians/Baptists (AUCECB) and the unregistered, illegal Council of Churches of Evangelical Christians/Baptists (CCECB). The Moiseyevs worship with a CCECB congregation.

Strelkov stood stamping his *valenki* in the snow and watching as Ivan ran across the field to his unit. In spite of his knee-length felt boots Strelkov's feet were getting cold, and he had missed his morning tea. It had not been a satisfactory interview. The other men had heard Moiseyev say he had prayed. The polit-officer would have to be notified.

The Polit-Ruk* office was poorly lit. The faint winter light that struggled to enter the room was in part blocked by limp green drapes that hung dispiritedly over the grimy glass. The polit-officer was Capt. Boris Zalivako, a hammer of a man, short and powerfully built with inscrutable bushy brows. A matter of unpunctuality was of no interest to him, but Strelkov's story, if it were not a poor joke of Moiseyev's, was.

Waiting for Moiseyev to arrive, Strelkov had misgivings. Perhaps he should not have taken Moiseyev seriously. He wished he had not conversed with him. He had hoped to give him some advice, to help him along. But it might well be that Moiseyev had made a fool of him. At least the men in formation could verify that he said he had been praying; he wouldn't be able to deny it. How many had actually heard him? Strelkov tried to remember who had been standing close enough to hear.

Captain Zalivako glanced lazily at Moiseyev standing at attention on the other side of the table. His side cap was at the proper angle. He had saluted correctly and with respect. Zalivako's interest was slightly stirred by the ease with which Moiseyev met his look. The young fellow was sure of himself, but there was no hint of insolence in his expression.

Zalivako motioned for him to sit down. "You don't look like the sort that would be late for a drill. What is the problem that you cannot manage to report on time with the rest of your unit?"

---

*The shortened term for *Politicheskoye-Rukovodstvo* ("Political-Directive" department).

"I am very sorry, comrade captain, for my tardiness. It won't happen again."

"You didn't answer my question. What explanation do you give for being late?" There was a tightening of Zalivako's voice. He disliked evasiveness.

"I was praying, sir." The answer hung in the air, almost visible in its strangeness.

Strelkov took a deep breath of relief. He had been quite right to report Moiseyev. Everyone knew religion was a menace to the Soviet way of life, in whatever harmless a form it might appear. Lenin himself had said that the goal of the Communist Party was to free the working masses from the idea of religion. Strelkov straightened himself conspicuously.

Zalivako tapped his fingers. "To whom were you praying?"

"To God, sir. The Creator of the universe, who loves all men."

"To God." Zalivako closed his eyes in a deep sigh. "It has been scientifically proven that God does not exist. Our Soviet scientists have studied this question thoroughly and they have verified the teachings of scientific communism that there is no God. The idea of God was invented by early man to explain economic conditions that could not be understood in primitive times."

"That is what atheists teach, sir."

"That is the correct view. That is the position of the Communist government, the Academy of Sciences, and every other great institution in Soviet life, including the Soviet Department of Defense. This is the position of the Soviet peoples."

"Comrade polit-officer, I know atheism is our official view. But the Bible teaches that God made man after He created the entire universe. This is the Christian belief."

Zalivako had been writing on the report sheet before him on his desk. He paused in his work. "You have a Bible?"

"No, sir."

"The Bible is not a welcome book in the Soviet Union. It is

full of unscientific errors of all kinds. It promotes passivity and subservience. It is not permitted in the army. In fact, I can't understand why anyone would read such a book."

"It changes lives, sir."

"The army changes lives, Moiseyev. And opinions. Perhaps you need assistance in realizing this. It is a far more profound truth than anything your Bible declares."

"I am eager to serve in the army to the best of my ability."

Zalivako began to be angry. Religious recruits were difficult to deal with. Believers were deceptive. Outwardly they appeared to be good citizens, quiet, peace-loving, harmless people. And under the cover of virtue, they spread their false teachings.

"I am happy to hear you say that, Moiseyev. Such a statement naturally means that you have decided to throw off your subversive ideas about God and enter fully into the program that has been planned to develop you as fully as possible into a Soviet soldier, unquestioning in your loyalty to the state. I congratulate you."

Strelkov glanced admiringly at Captain Zalivako. The Polit-Ruk knew how to handle men. But Zalivako was continuing, ignoring the distress on Moiseyev's face. "I will take special interest in your political development and in your participation in the full range of military and political activities required of you."

Zalivako rose from his chair, watching Moiseyev intently as he waited for his response. The boy would be a fool not to take the exit he had been given. But believers were fools to start with. He wished Moiseyev's Russian were better. It was tiresome to listen to his halting speech.

"I am happy as a Soviet citizen to serve in the army and to help build socialism in any way I can. But there is another place of which I am a citizen, and that is the Kingdom of God. It is a Kingdom that can never be a threat to the Soviet state because this Kingdom is within the hearts of believers, and the laws of this place are the laws of love. I cannot renounce my citizenship

38

in this Kingdom or my loyalty to the King, who is God. He is building His Kingdom everywhere, even in the Soviet Union, a Kingdom of forgiveness and love."

Zalivako's voice began to shake as he answered. "We have done away with kingdoms in the Soviet Union, Moiseyev, and with kings! Perhaps in your zeal you have somehow forgotten that fact. We have places only for those loyal to the Soviet state, nothing else!"

Strelkov was deflated. He had hoped to see a demonstration of how smoothly these matters could be handled. And it was incredible to him that any Soviet youth could have been so thoroughly poisoned by religion.

But Zalivako was not finished. "It is evident that you resist teaching, Moiseyev, and the advice of your superiors. That is a concern to me. You are in need of a lesson. Since you are fond of praying on your knees, I shall give you an opportunity for constructive socialist labor in that position. You are to wash the barrack's drill hall and all the corridors on your knees with a bucket and brush. You will work all night. Perhaps an exercise of this nature, and before your comrades, might help to persuade you to be teachable. You will have opportunity to consider if you wish to cling to your anti-Soviet views. Dismissed."

Strelkov stood smartly to attention, saluting Captain Zalivako. The matter had been brought to a satisfactory conclusion. A good feeling passed briefly between the two men as Moiseyev saluted and left the room. Such degrading labor would teach Moiseyev what knees were for.

Before the pale December sun had climbed halfway to the top of the frozen sky the news of a believer in the unit had passed through the whole company. Smiles appeared as the story spread from man to man with heads shaking or shoulders shrugging in amusement or disinterest. Fast upon the first story came the second, that the Polit-Ruk had set Moiseyev to scrubbing the enormous barrack hall with a small hand brush and a bucket. Incredibly, he was in good humor, singing and smiling as he worked in spite of continuous interruptions by officers who called him into their offices to harass him. By lunch, soldiers were drifting into the hall on their way to the dining rooms, watching him work, listening to the quiet hymns he sang with such evident joy. He was a mystery.

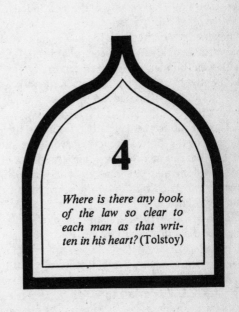

4

Where is there any book of the law so clear to each man as that written in his heart? (Tolstoy)

Kerch, the colorful Ukraine seaport in the lush strait jutting into the Black Sea, was an exciting place to a young soldier of limited travels. Ivan strained his eyes as he bumped along in the back of the troop transport truck. In the distance he could see the streaming smokestacks of the iron and steel mills. Close by, the smell of the glittering sea and the screams of seagulls quickened his enthusiasm for new sights. This city was a very old one, the soldiers had been told in a preliminary briefing. It had been founded in the sixth century by the Greeks and called Panticapaeum. The soldiers were to observe the highest hill in the city, named Mithradates. On it still stood the crumbling Greek ruins of an acropolis.

The acropolis, the officer had informed the young men, was the seat of the Greek "soviet." It would be interesting to them that in Kerch the glorious Soviet traditions of human dignity and freedom that had only truly begun with the Revolution were now carried out under the very shadow of the Greek acropolis itself.

That was all very well, Ivan was to reflect later. But it was at the new base in Kerch that his testings began in earnest.

For the first few days he was free to join the streams of soldiers hurrying in every direction, chatting quietly, their briefcases swollen with books and papers. He felt refreshed and lighthearted. Often in fitness drills, in classroom lectures, in military training sessions he prayed, "Lord, let me excel in this. Let me be a good soldier for Your glory."

Ivan had hoped that after leaving Odessa the interrogations would cease. He was as glad to be gone as Zalivako was to have him gone. But Zalivako had been thorough in sending an alert to the Kerch Polit-Ruk about the presence of a believer in Unit 61968T. Private Moiseyev had admitted openly that he prayed, was a Baptist believer, and would attend meetings of believers whenever he had the opportunity. He had stubbornly withstood vigorous indoctrination and refused to be silent about his beliefs.

Hardly two weeks had passed before reports of barracks discussions began to reach the Kerch Polit-Ruk office. The decree of Lenin, point 5, gave members of cults free celebration of religious rites, but not the right to propagate religion, which infringed upon the freedom of other citizens. Why couldn't Moiseyev understand? Ivan tried to explain to the polit-officers that the men in his unit often asked him about Christ. If they wanted to know about salvation, where was the law that said he could not answer their questions? How could he refuse them? All believers are to be witnesses.

And if it were not a command of Christ to share His love, how would it be possible to hide the joy that met Ivan at every turn? A leaf falling from the frozen sky was God's touch. The sudden remembrance of a forgotten Scripture was God's voice. The blasts of wind spoke of God's power, the moon His beauty, the strength of his own body was God's strength poured into him.

Junior Polit-Officer Captain Yarmak was young and restless. He itched for a challenge that would help him to rise in the party structure. All the better if Moiseyev were difficult. His success with him would look doubly good on his record. Yarmak took his responsibilities seriously. Every one of the eleven hundred soldiers at Kerch must be totally committed to the Communist Party and the teachings of scientific atheism. Only then could the military be assured of the total and immediate obedience that was required of every Soviet soldier. Decisively, he raised his eyes from the papers on his desk as Moiseyev was brought before him. He stared for several seconds before speaking, changing his expression to match the harshness in his voice. "Have you ever been sick, Moiseyev?"

He was gratified to see Moiseyev's surprise.

"No sir, I've never even seen the inside of a hospital."

Yarmak folded his arms dramatically. The brass buttons on his cuff caught the light in a way that pleased him. Political development was so often a matter of shock offensive.

"It is fortunate you are well. You will be needing a strong constitution for the next few days—or a change of mind, which seems to be so difficult for you." He paused for the maximum effect. "You showed an unsound and rebellious attitude in Odessa. Attempts have been made to persuade you to renounce your anti-Soviet views and to increase your military and political knowledge. But you refuse. Until you agree to submit yourself to the authority of this base and to obey the orders given to you, you will be confined without meals. Dismissed."

The room to which Ivan was taken was not a cell but a detention room used by the polit-officers for questioning and confinement. A cot, covered with the regulation-gray army blanket, a table, three chairs, and some army manuals on a shelf made up the furnishings. In a corner was a filthy toilet beside a tap. The large window was barred and the double doors locked twice. The room was very cold, bathed in a pale late afternoon light.

For Ivan, it was a chapel. Thankfully he sank down on the cot, his head whirling with the faces of angry officers from Odessa and Kerch fading and dissolving like scenes from a military film. What bliss to sleep and to awake to pray!

Many times before, the Lord had called Ivan to periods of fasting and supplication. Ivan smiled at the holy joke. In such times he had been greatly strengthened and refreshed. Captain Yarmak couldn't have given him a greater gift. Full of gratitude, Ivan turned his attention to the Lord, to seek Him in prayer and fasting. How long he would fast was in God's hand, not Yarmak's.

The second night he was awakened by a distant, rhythmic pounding. He lay trying to distinguish the sound when a key was turned in the lock. Yellow light splashed into the room. An officer Ivan did not know stood in the doorway. Without turning on the light he spoke to the dark room.

"You're wanted in the lecture room at the end of the hall. Come at once." The noise of his boots faded rapidly in the long corridor.

Ivan struggled to rouse himself fully as he saw the elite group of officers waiting to question him. He focused his eyes on the electric wall clock. Two-fifteen in the morning. Most of the officers were sprawled informally in the desk seats, smoking and sipping from steaming mugs of tea. Sometimes they would speak quietly, asking a question and waiting for his reply. At other times shouts would suddenly come from different officers in a rapid fire of accusations and statements.

Was he not ill? Had he changed his attitude? His ideas were imperialist, relics of czarism and capitalism. His ideas could not be tolerated in the Red army. He need not think he was suffering anything for his beliefs. He was being disciplined for avoiding his obligations to the army. How long was he going to evade his responsibilities to his comrades and to the Soviet state? Supposing God exists, could He then make a space too small for Himself? Why did he deliberately withhold food from himself? He was creating questions concerning his mental stability. Did he not understand that a rejection of Marxist-Leninist teaching was a rejection of the Soviet way of life? God was created by man to explain famine and disease and economic conditions he was too primitive to understand. The idea of God was no longer necessary. It impeded the development of the free socialist citizen. People who propagated such ideas were enemies of the Soviet state.

At all times of his fasting, Ivan was called for interrogation sessions, sometimes at night before several officers, sometimes before polit-officers, once or twice before an officer who would begin in a fatherly manner and very quickly continue in abusive shouting.

It was five days before the testing came to an end. On the last morning, in a tumult of argumentative voices and clatter of equipment, an ancient x-ray machine was wheeled into the hall to the doorway of the detention room. Ivan could hear a furious controversy ensuing as to the size of the doors and whether they would admit the machine. In the end, Ivan was thrust into the hall to have an x-ray made of his digestive tract. The technician, a Jew from Estonia named Myakaev, was sputtering with frustration. This clearly was not a medical matter. To bring him out in the cold, all the way over from the hospital, and to expect a machine to operate properly after bumping it up and down ramps and over icy broken pavements was criminal negligence of socialist property.

Later in the day Captain Yarmak entered the room, the x-ray and a report sheet in his hand. As if the question had not already been asked a hundred times, he sat quietly in one of the wooden chairs and looked closely at Ivan as he spoke. "Well, Moiseyev, have you changed your mind? Five days without food have passed."

The captain seemed smaller and farther away than the few feet his chair was distant from Ivan's cot. Ivan was tired, but he tried to concentrate on Yarmak's question and his own answer.

"One night I was praying." he began. "I was rather cold and wishing for sleep because I had been awakened twice that night. But I was awake and praying to God for my family and friends, and for you, Captain Yarmak, as well."

Yarmak stood up impatiently and gazed at the snow falling behind the bars of the window.

"It wasn't as if I was especially conscious of being hungry, but I was very tired and certainly cold. As I prayed, God suddenly touched me in a wonderful way. I was warmed and felt as full as if I had eaten a large and delicious dinner. Soon

46

afterward I fell asleep. When I awoke, it was morning with the sun streaming in the window. A bird was outside on the sill, singing. There is a Scripture that says, 'Call upon Me in the day of trouble; I shall rescue you, and you will honor Me.' It is because of God's rescue that I am not hungry or sick. How can I possibly 'change my mind'? You can look at me and see for yourself what God has done."

Yarmak stared at the swirling flakes of snow, his mind a turmoil of anger. As a political leader his position depended on success with men like Moiseyev. Already Colonel Malsin had sent him a memo. "Let Moiseyev eat. I don't want to be blamed if he dies of starvation because of you." With freezing dignity, Yarmak left the room.

It was during the morning long-distance running that Ivan met Sergei. A thick fog had rolled in from the Black Sea, obscuring the barren trees that were landmarks for the drill. Until the unit reached the maximum distance of fifteen kilometers before breakfast, the course was being lengthened each day, forcing the men to the outer limits of their endurance. Across rigid fields, down gulleys, jumping ditches half-hidden in the fog, the men ran in growing agony. It was as if the landscape itself was grunting with effort, the thudding of hidden feet throbbing like a painful heartbeat beneath the crust of frozen snow.

Ivan was lagging, trying to pace himself carefully and ignore the terrible thirst that tore at his throat. Gradually he became aware of a soldier from another unit keeping pace beside him. The soldier suddenly shouted in a hoarse gasp, "He is risen!"

What had he said? Ivan tried to fit phrases into the rhythm of the words. Perhaps, "Will it blizzard?"

A light wind was blowing at the smoking fog. Ivan turned to see the soldier's face. It was gray with effort but strained in a smile. Again he shouted. "I said, 'He is risen,' brother! He—is—risen!"

It was as if the frozen earth had tipped up from behind and Ivan was suddenly running downhill in a flood of joy. With a yell that was almost a whoop he responded to the ancient Easter greeting. "He is risen indeed! Hallelujah!" The greeting of embrace would wait till later.

The place they found to meet was one of the large garages for army vehicles that flanked the front gate of the base. It was an old stone building that had once been used to stable horses. Before that, and during the war, it was said to be a barrack. Its thick walls kept out the worst of the cold, and the wide parking aisles made ideal paths for walking and praying. Occasionally another soldier or two would duck into the building to have a cigarette out of the wind, but in general Ivan and Sergei were undisturbed in the few minutes they could find to be together.

Such meetings were infrequent in the relentless pace of army life. But the knowledge of Sergei's presence on the base was encouragement enough. Meeting a brother unconsciously lulled Ivan into a feeling that all would be well, after all. It was with an unpleasant shock that he received a summons to report to Maj. Alexander Petrovich Gidenko in the Polit-Ruk.

5

*A saint sleeps not
on soft beds.*

Major Gidenko was a huge man with a leonine face and military stance that set off his height. As a youth he had excelled in athletics, and the awards and prizes he had won had made him a favorite of his teachers and classmates. Russia had been good to him, and the fact that he had been born in the same year as the Revolution gave him a sense of destiny that had inspired courage in his difficult university studies. From university, he had made the army his life. As head of Kerch's Political-Directive Committee he was determined that this problem with Moiseyev be resolved before the Polit-Ruk commissar for the Crimea would have to be brought in.

Gidenko sighed. He had been in the army thirty-two years and had seen every kind of man come and go, but he had never understood the *religiozniks*. To him they were merely half-hearted creatures creeping around the backstairs of Soviet life. Why did they not renounce their strange practices and enter fully into the life of the Soviet state, contributing fully as they should and fully reaping the benefits?

The great Patriotic War had been the climax of Gidenko's life. As a young soldier in the Battle of Stalingrad, he had stared horrified at the guns of fascist troops a hundred meters away. A conviction that he would never survive the battle had gripped him. The Nazi atrocities he had witnessed had weakened his will to live; he felt he was going blind from the snow and the glare of the sun on his comrades' white uniforms. Under shellfire he had dashed to the party headquarters in the corner of a bombed mill and had joined the Communist Party. He had carried his party card into battle. That he survived only deepened his sense of destiny. He was born and lived to serve Russia.

That people could cling to the idea of God was incomprehensible. Perhaps the old were too fearful to change, but how could a young person take such folklore seriously—even in its most harmless form? Moiseyev had been properly educated in socialist schools. He had been taught the depravity of religion, the decaying influence that Christianity had had upon Russia with its corrupt priests and churchmen land-owners.

A cold wind whipped across the snow fields stretching out for miles beyond the base. Gidenko sighed again.

He had dealt many times with believers. Experience had taught him that effectiveness was often not so much a matter of persuasion or political reeducation, although he believed in trying. It was very often a matter of discipline.

"When you think of it," he had ruefully smiled at his wife over his plate of steaming cabbage soup the night before, "for all our programs on scientific atheism, we succeed in changing the opinions of very few believers. Severe punishment too often is the only recourse. I could just as well close down the Polit-Ruk if we had to depend on indoctrination alone."

Yet he would be responsible to Colonel Malsin for this Moiseyev, one way or another.

It was a long walk to Major Gidenko's office, and as Ivan strode along the shoveled streets of the base, he was giving praise to God for the time to pray. A Scripture verse his small brother Ilyusha had taught him to sing at home was in his mind, and he sang it softly, keeping time with its music while he walked. "The joy of the Lord is your strength. The joy of the Lord is your strength. The joy of the Lord is your strength." The tune was light-hearted and fit the brightness of the sun on the snow.

It was a clear day. Something flashed and glittered in the sky overhead. "The joy of the Lord is your strength." Joy was filling him. The trees in the small park in the central square of the base seemed dusted with a heavenly light. Ivan saluted every passing tree in Jesus' name. The light was dazzling, like sunlight on a mirror. He lifted his eyes upward at the same instant that he heard a voice, "Vanya. Vanya."

The angel was above him with a brightness and presence that caught terror in the joy and held both sensations motionless in his heart.

The voice was like a memory, unmistakable, clear, and strangely wordless. "Do not be afraid." Through the transparent form of the angel Ivan could see the large trees on the opposite side of the park. The form of the angel seemed to be moving. Staring, Ivan slowly resumed walking. The radiance of the angel lit the park far more brightly than the sun. But he was speaking again.

"Do not be afraid. Go. I am with you." There were no words in which Ivan could reply. His joy was like a fire within him. Or perhaps the warmth came from the angel's light. How he came to the door of Major Gidenko's building he was later to wonder. But as the brightness faded the sense of presence did not. He made his way to the major's office and knocked quietly on the door. Gidenko smiled at Ivan expansively. This would be easier than he thought. What was the matter with Yarmak? If he didn't know Moiseyev's age, he would have guessed sixteen. The lad had a farm-boy face. "Sit down, son." With an open palm he gestured to the leather chair on the opposite side of his desk. There was a gentleness about him.

"You're a long way from Moldavia, Moiseyev."

"Yes, sir."

"After a year, you'll have leave."

"Yes, sir."

"Miss your family? Mother, father?"

"I do, sir."

"I remember my first days in the army. I used to write home every day. Seems funny, now. You write home a lot?"

"Not so much as every day, sir. I don't have time."

"No? Why not?"

"The interrogations, sir. I spend a great deal of my time being questioned at the Polit-Ruk."

"And these questionings. Are you not learning the correct answers? You don't look like a poor pupil to me."

"Sometimes there is a difference between the correct answers and the true ones. Sometimes God does not permit me to give 'correct' answers."

"Indeed? And who is this God of yours?" As soon as the question was out, Gidenko regretted it. Moiseyev was leaning forward in his chair, his face alight with opportunity.

"Sir, He is the Creator of all the universe. He is a spirit and greatly loves man . . . ."

"Yes, yes. I know the Christian teaching." Gidenko shifted in his chair. "These correct answers that you cannot give: is it because they are untrue? You disagree with the teaching of the glorious Red army?"

"No, sir."

"But you do not accept the principles of scientific atheism upon which is based our entire Soviet state and the military power of the army?"

"I cannot accept what I know to be untrue. Everything else I can gladly accept."

"It is not possible to prove the existence of God. Even religious people agree to that. Priests and pastors agree to that."

Ivan could hear the warmth die out of the major's voice. He began to pray in his spirit before answering.

Gidenko pressed his point. "You see, even your own teachers do not talk as you talk—about *knowing* God."

"Sir, they speak about proving God. There is no question about knowing Him. He is with me now, in this room. Before I came here He sent an angel to encourage me."

Gidenko stared intently at Ivan. Was the boy pretending to be simple-minded? Was his behavior a ruse to be discharged from active service? There was a simpleness about him. A deliberate simpleness!

He rose massively from his chair. "Moiseyev, we have had men in the army before like you. No doubt there will always be one or two." He averted his eyes from the sudden look of pleasure that appeared in Ivan's face. Gidenko was becoming convinced that Moiseyev was not a dangerous *religioznik* but a homesick boy desperate for a leave. He had seen games like Moiseyev's played before. And hadn't the lad gone without food five days and pretended he wasn't hungry? Gidenko had seen soldiers who pretended not to understand when food was placed before them. A visit to the psychiatrist had cured their pretended mental illness!

But there was no question as to Moiseyev's sanity. He was too simple even to lie well.

When Gidenko spoke, it was wearily. "I am sorry, Moiseyev, that you persist in your irregular behavior. It will achieve nothing for you except discomfort. However, I feel you will come to your senses with a little discipline and be cured of your delusions of angels and talking gods. I am going to order you to stand in the street tonight after taps are played until you are willing to come to me and apologize for the nonsense you have been circulating around the base about yourself and your so-called experiences with God. Since the temperature is likely to be some twenty-five degrees below zero,* for your sake, I hope you quickly agree to behave sensibly. Tomorrow we shall make a plan together for your political reeducation. You are dismissed."

Gidenko was unaccountably irritated by the courage with which Moiseyev seemed to take the order. He had expected a hesitation, a reconsidering, but Moiseyev's face was quiet and his shoulders squared as he walked the correct pace to the door.

---

*-25° Centigrade is equivalent to -13° Fahrenheit.

"Comrade private!"

Ivan turned. Gidenko observed he was a trifle pale. He *had* understood the order, then.

"You will obey my instructions in summer uniform. That is all."

The aging corporal in the quartermaster corps was incredulous at Ivan's requisition for the issue of a summer uniform. Was not the snow already two feet in the fields? He studied the order in bewilderment, his wrinkled hand rubbing his chin pensively. It didn't seem, somehow, that the order could be correct. He didn't want to be blamed if something was wrong. What was the use of a summer uniform in winter? What was it wanted for? Ivan's explanation brought an expression of craft to his crow-footed eyes. A joke was being played on him, and he'd end up on the short end of it, too.

A brusque telephone verification from the Polit-Ruk sped the light trousers, shirt, jacket, and side cap into Ivan's hands. The corporal was silent, handing the articles to Ivan with a grave shaking of his white head. Ivan could almost hear the labored thoughts behind the sympathetic eyes. It was to be a bitter night.

A wind came up as the moon rose, lifting powdery snow from the corners of the buildings and swirling it across the well-swept streets. It was already cold in the barracks as the soldiers undressed for the night, huddling in their bunks under the heavy blankets for warmth.

Igor Alexandrovich Markov leaned against the wall, swathed in his blanket, smoking a Kazbek cigarette. From Georgia, he had the luminous dark eyes and black hair of his homeland and the easy temperament. Moiseyev was a mystery to him, and he gazed wonderingly as Ivan changed into the summer uniform.

"Tell me again, Moiseyev, what you're doing." The low conversations in the bunks within hearing distance became hushed. On the bunk above Ivan's, Vladimir Yakovlevich Albu coughed suddenly, hiding a smile.

Ivan was getting tired of telling his story. The news of this new punishment had spread like wildfire through the mess hall at supper. The private assigned to ladeling the soup at his table had heard the account from the quartermaster corporal, and he distributed the news with every bowl of borscht. Ivan had been questioned or admonished at least a dozen times as he made his way out of the hall after supper.

And his answer sounded absurd. "At taps I am to report to the duty officer and stand outside in the street." He didn't blame the men for smiling. If the Polit-Ruk wanted to make a public example of Ivan, they were succeeding. Now, the men listening to Ivan and Igor jumped into the conversation. "How long are you going to stay out in the cold?" "You will have to give in. You will die of the cold." "Why do you refuse to be quiet about religion?" "Why can you not believe and be silent?" "You will be inside after five minutes."

Igor raised his voice above the others, quieting them. "Ivan! Why? What is it that you believe, that you would do this?"

"I believe God wants men to know that He exists, and loves man, and came in the form of Jesus Christ, as a real man, to this earth. It is almost Christmas. At this time we believers celebrate the coming of Christ to Bethlehem as a baby. All over the world, believers observe this great thing that God did and give glory to God. I believe He came to die for the sin of every man who wants forgiveness. For me. For you too, Igor."

Demchenko, a Komsomol enthusiast a few bunks down, interrupted loudly. "I don't think we want to be listening to this talk, comrades. I for one am not interested. I am surprised it has appeal for anyone. Especially Comrade Markov!"

There was a snicker from Vladimir Yakovlevich as the small group broke up. "Igor's not interested! Christmas talk is all right for the Baptists, maybe. But not Igor! He's too fond of his cigarettes and vodka!"

There was perfunctory laughter from the bunks cut suddenly

short. In the distance the soft notes of a bugle could be heard. The light was immediately switched off. Hurrying, Ivan made his way to the door. From the window the brilliant moon lit the aisle between the bunks as he passed. There was silence behind him as he made his way down the stairs and to the street outside.

At first the cold was a shock slamming into his face with an impact that left his head aching and his eyes full of water. He recoiled from the icy wind that burned at his ears. He knew faces at the darkened barracks windows would be peering into the street. The moon lit the road and the snowbanks against the buildings. He stiffened against the freezing blast, glancing at his watch. It was one minute after ten o'clock.

He would have a long time to pray. He began haltingly, a slow fear rising in him that he tried to push away. How long *could* he stand out here? What if he became so cold he gave in? What if he froze to death? Would they let him freeze to death? He tried to concentrate on praying, but a panic constricted his chest. How long would it take to freeze to death? Would it be quick? What if he were *almost* frozen by morning but revived? He had heard the pain of frozen limbs was terrible. What if they had to amputate? He had to get his mind off it. He began to sing. "The joy of the Lord is your strength. The joy of the Lord is your strength."

Suddenly the glory of the morning revisited him. He looked at the park in the central square, distant in the moonlight but visible. An angelic light seemed to linger upon it. "Do not be afraid. I am with you!" The angel's words! They had been for tonight! Even the warmth of those moments seemed to resettle upon him. Fervently Ivan opened his mouth and softly began to pray.

It was twelve-thirty when his attention was distracted by the crunching of steps in the snow. Bundled in their greatcoats, three officers slowly were making their way toward him from the barrack.

Their voices were gruff and almost blown away by the wind.

"Well, Moiseyev, have you reconsidered? Are you ready to come in? Have you had enough of standing out here?"

Even in the moonlight Ivan could see that they were looking at him with a measure of apprehension. Was it possible that he was warm?

"Thank you, comrade officers. I would like very much to come in and go to bed. But I cannot agree to remain silent about God."

"Then you're going to stand out here all night long?" Each of their faces was twinged with fear.

"I'd rather not. But I don't see how anything else is possible, and God is helping me." Ivan was rubbing his hands with his fingertips as he stood at attention. Excitement shook his voice. His hands were cold, but no colder than they had been while dressing in the barracks. He tentatively wiggled his toes. They moved easily, without discomfort. A feeling of astonishment grew in him. He looked at the officers in excitement. He could see that even in their coats they were cold. They were stamping their feet and slapping their hands, shifting their weight, impatient to return to their heater in the barracks. He would feel differently in another hour, the senior officer mumbled as they wheeled away. Ivan couldn't resist a wondering laugh.

Soon the surge of relief subsided and a feeling of brokenness took its place. He was no better than any of the young people in his congregation at home. His parents had suffered in difficult situations for years. He knew of pastors who had been questioned, arrested, even sent to prison camps. Yet he was touched again and again by God's direct power and deliverance. Something in him pulled away from such magnificent singling-out. He didn't want to be special, he didn't deserve miracles and mysteries. He *ought* to be freezing. He wasn't good enough. Hot tears rimmed his eyes.

By three o'clock in the morning he was dozing on his feet. His prayers of repentance were long over. His intercessions for all the believers he knew he had made over and over. He had sung Christmas carols. He had prayed for every officer he knew and knew of. He had cried out to God on behalf of the men in his unit. But gradually his mind seemed to be floating somewhere outside of his head. As much as he tried to command prayer, it eluded him.

Suddenly a voice in his ear startled him fully awake. The senior officer on duty was speaking gently.

"All right, Moiseyev, you are to come inside." The moon had set and the wind died down, and in the pitch-black, Ivan strained to see his face. The officer hesitated, standing still beside Ivan, the yellow light from the barracks caught in the gold oak-ieaf insignia of his hat. His voice was intense. "What kind of person are you?"

"Sir?"

"What kind of person are you that the cold does not bother you?"

Ivan also spoke softly. "Oh, comrade, I am a person just like you. But I prayed to God and was warm."

The officer turned and began walking very slowly back to the barracks, touching Ivan's arm as a signal to accompany him. "Tell me about this God," he said.

Major Gidenko was profoundly disturbed. The report to Colonel Malsin concerning Ivan Moiseyev defied reason. For twelve nights in a row he had stood in sub-zero weather in a summer uniform. It was impossible that he did not freeze and beg for mercy. Last night Gidenko himself had gone to see him. It was true that his face was blue with cold and he had been swaying with fatigue. The powdery snow, lifted by the wind, had dusted his hair and uniform so that he looked frighteningly like a statue. But he was composed and not as cold after four hours as Gidenko was in five minutes. Was it possible that a young man could endure weather like that and not feel it? Well, it was possible, of course. Moiseyev had done it for two weeks. Gidenko was more disturbed than he had been in years. He had not slept well recently. Something would have to be put in the report for Malsin and the Polit-

Ruk district commissar. It was clear that the punishment was not effective. The whole base was talking about Moiseyev. He would have to order a stop to these public vigils.

6

*Fear not the law,
but the judge.*

Although the regulation bunk beds were only two feet wide and hard, Ivan stretched out between sheets and beneath a blanket and thanked God for the luxury. For the first time in 1971 he was in bed. No hours in the cold. No interrogations in the snow, in the officer's rooms. No watching the moon set behind the tiny park in the central square. Even before taps were sounded, Ivan was blissfully asleep.

Although he had only heard it once before, the Voice was so familiar Ivan was instantly awake. "Vanya, arise!" In a second he was on his feet between the bunks gazing at the crystal brilliance of the angel. His mind was working rapidly. He was aware that no sleeping soldier in the rows of bunks stirred. Mechanically he began to pull on his trousers and feel for his shoes, his eyes never leaving the radiant loveliness of the being before him. The angel's gaze was so full of love he felt no fear. In an instant they began to rise, and effortlessly the ceiling opened, and then the barrack's roof, and Ivan and the angel flew through time and space to another world.

The grass was deep and lush and seemed to stretch to the very horizon of this unfamiliar planet. It was a fresh and vivid green. Dazed, Ivan followed the angel, and after what seemed a long time they came to a brook. Its waters were as clear as glass so Ivan could see to the bed of the stream, and the brightness of the water dazzled his eyes. The angel passed over the brook without effort and turned questioningly when Ivan held back.

"Why do you fear, Vanya?" The voice was unhurried and tender. Inexplicably a horror of snakes had entered Ivan's mind.

"Snakes." As he said the word his glance moved through thick grass under his feet. The strangeness of what was happening gripped him in an unreasoning fear.

62

Although the angel was a distance from him, Ivan heard his voice as if the shining creature were standing by his side. "Do not be afraid. You are with me. Here it is not as on the earth. Here there are no snakes."

As suddenly as it had come, the fear left him, and Ivan moved easily over the brook. In the brilliance of this world, every detail of blade of grass and petal of flower stood out as if floodlit. The patterns of the bark upon the trees were indescribably beautiful. The expanse of the branches were profoundly graceful, so luminous that the light seemed to pour from within each tree. Instinctively Ivan lifted his eyes to the sky, gazing in every direction. There was no sun.

When his eyes returned to the angel there was a form beside the being, more exalted and at the same time somehow more loving in his brilliance than even the angel. In some way the angel seemed to do him deference, and Ivan knew him to be the apostle John. Through the angel, the apostle communicated with him. Ivan stood transfixed, his mind absorbing every holy word. A series of three beings followed the apostle, recognized in some mysterious way by Ivan to be David, Moses, and Daniel. So intense was Ivan's concentration and so overwhelming his awe and joy that when the last form was gone Ivan felt he would fall into a deep sleep. But the angel, now alone in the streaming light, spoke again.

"We have traveled a long way and you are tired. Come and sit."

The tree under which Ivan sat was large and welcoming with a fragrance that reminded him in some unexplained way of the grape fields of Moldavia. If the angel had not spoken again Ivan felt he would be content to sit forever, smelling the tree and looking at the landscape in the sparkling light.

"I wish to show you the heavenly city, the new Jerusalem. But if you see it as it is, you cannot remain in the body you now have. And there is still much work for you left on earth." There seemed a silence before the angel resumed speaking. "We will fly together to another planet and I will show you the light of this city for you to know, while you are yet alive in your earth body, that in certainty there is a new Jerusalem."

In an instant they flew to another planet where there were high mountains. Again, the glory of the light illuminated every detail of this world. Ivan's gaze rested on diamond streams coursing down the mountain slopes into mists that rose from vividly green valleys. When they had come to a very deep canyon, the angel and Ivan descended until they were at the bottom.

The angel seemed a flame of joy, the Voice more ceremonious and jubilant than Ivan had yet heard it. "Vanya, look upward and you will see this light of the new Jerusalem."

At the first glance Ivan recoiled in dismay. The brilliance was so intense that even though he had seen it only for a second, he was sure he had been blinded. The angel spoke immediately. "Nothing will happen to you. Look."

No man rescued from a desert ever drank water more thirstily than Ivan drank in the splendor of that light. So great was its power it could be felt, tasted, heard. The sight of it was not a sensation of his eyes but of his whole being. Ivan could have wept with grief and disappointment when the angel said, "The time has come to fly back to earth."

At the instant that Ivan's feet touched the floor beside his bunk, three things happened. The angel disappeared, the bugle for reveille sounded, and the lights in the room were snapped on. Staring stupidly at his neat bed and himself fully dressed, Ivan heard a gentle laugh from the bunk beside him. Grigorii Fedorovich Chernykh, his neighbor, was also a Moldavian and took a fraternal interest in his strange countryman. Now Chernykh was pulling himself expertly out of his bunk and shoving his feet into trouser legs as he whispered in a conspiratorial tone. "Vanya, where were you last night?"

With a tremendous effort Ivan pulled his thoughts together. The barrack was alive with bodies hurtling past his bunk to the door. Good-natured bantering, the groaning of exhausted soldiers, the flash of uniforms seemed unreal. He turned to look intently at Chernykh.

"You don't mean that you didn't see me getting undressed and into bed last night? We turned in at the same time."

Chernykh was buttoning his shirt rapidly. "You went to bed the same time as I did, all right, and to sleep, too. But you didn't sleep long. I woke up about three A.M. and your bunk was empty. Vanya, you were nowhere in this room." Reaching for his jacket, he gave Ivan a sly smile. "Of all people, did you actually go A.W.O.L. last night?"

He had not been dreaming! He *had* journeyed with the angel! Excitement tore through Ivan like electricity. They were moving hurriedly to the door.

His voice shook as he spoke. "Let's ask the duty officer if anyone left during the night."

The duty officer was indignant. "Certainly no one left the room. Get going! Are you trying to get me arrested?"

Ivan and Grigorii Chernykh moved out into the morning, both in silence. Finally Chernykh broke the spell of strangeness with a question, and Ivan began to tell him about the angel.

By that evening, Ivan's account had spread through the unit. Nobody believed it, Chernykh thought with satisfaction. In spite of Ivan's sincerity, his stories were impossible. Yet they contained a mystery that made everyone uncomfortable. How was it possible to go five days without food and not be ill? How could a man stand in below-zero frost for hours and not be cold? And if Ivan Vasilievich had not left the barracks all night, yet was not in the room, where did he go?

Chernykh stretched on his bunk. Four hours of free time a month was too precious to waste on daydreaming. He reached for a pencil and paper. He would write home. But he remained on his back, staring at the ceiling.

Perhaps the Polit-Ruk would get to the bottom of it. For a full month they had been relentlessly questioning Ivan until

Grigorii wondered how he could remain sane under the pressure. For most men, army life was a merciless ordeal as it was. They were kept in a run all day long from the six A.M. reveille to the ten P.M. taps. And when they all should have been sleeping, there were the night battle alarms. How they dreaded the siren in the early hours of the morning that pulled them out of bed and propelled them, half-conscious, into a simulated enemy attack in the frozen night. Chernykh had a score to settle with the army for what had happened at the last alarm. Snow had been falling so thickly he had been unable to see the way. Straining his eyes to peer through the swirling snow he had plunged into an open well. Shouting over the wind and the snow and hanging onto the sides of the well for his life, Grigorii had been dragged out by a fellow soldier. With the water freezing on his *valenki,* his trouser legs stiff as cement, he had gone through the maneuvers shaking violently with the cold.

But they were never awakened only once in a night. Speechless with cold and exhaustion, the men would fall into their bunks only to be aroused again an hour or so later to repeat the whole pandemonium. Grigorii had lost count, but from his initial furious records (he had intended to produce them for his family on his first leave) he knew the alarms were sounded every second or third night. It was unscientific to expect men to train and study the next day on three or four hours' sleep.

How Ivan Vasilievich bore up under the constant interrogations in addition to the regular schedule Grigorii could not imagine. He had seen Ivan summoned from meals, from study periods, from sleep. Day or night, it didn't matter. Ivan's bunk was often empty these nights.

He was in trouble, all right. There had been too many incidents, too many unexplainable happenings. Perhaps Chernykh didn't agree that the Baptists were enemies of the state. But it was certain they were fanatical and foolish. One didn't argue with the Red army. It was hopeless to think one could withstand. If an officer said cabbages were sunflowers, they were sunflowers.

In a way, perhaps it came down to a question of obedience. Perhaps that was why the Polit-Ruk was dealing so decisively with Moiseyev. After all, in a maneuver, where would any of them be if one of them wouldn't obey orders? Chernykh stretched again in his bunk, the paper and pencil for his letter still idle on the coarse blanket. He had heard from one of the men in his unit that the commissar for the whole Crimean Polit-Ruk was visiting Colonel Malsin. There was talk that Moiseyev would be sent to the military detention center in Sverdlovsk in the Urals. With a determination to put it out of his mind, Chernykh seized his pencil. It had nothing to do with him. It certainly was not related to *his* telling the men Ivan's story about going up to another planet with an angel. Ivan spoke openly to anyone about God or His angels. Writing furiously, Chernykh tried to forget. Last evening, walking back to the barracks from a field drill, he had been afraid to look deeply into the night sky.

The landscape had long withdrawn into winter as the train jolted from side to side along the icy tracks. Fields, woods, small lakes, ravines glided past the half-open sliding door of the special railway car used for military prisoners. Wooden benches were piled in a shelf formation along the sides and center of the car where the prisoners sat or slept in the airless dusk, some quarreling, some chatting, most wrapped in their own bitter thoughts.

Ivan stayed close to the partially open door, breathing in the cold air and ignoring the arguments that sprang up from time to time about the door's closing or remaining open. A sense of deep peace pervaded the sweep of the land that drifted dreamlike before his view. The guard, a private from a base outside of Moscow, leaned against the shuddering walls of the car, his gun slung loosely over his arm, his head nodding in sleep. Waves of irritability rippled over the crowd of prisoners, came to nothing, and ebbed away. Ivan felt himself to be suspended between the mixture of soldiers behind him in the car and the remote countryside.

His mind reviewed his attempts to demonstrate his determination to be a good soldier. In his political sessions, he had made a point of explaining that the Bible taught believers to love the country in which they live, to respect its authorities, and to give them all that is due.

Instead of success, his efforts had resulted in his being pulled out of his bunk in the middle of the night and driven over frozen back roads to the prison train bound for Sverdlovsk, a military prison two thousand kilometers in the direction of Siberia.

They had left the plains of central Russia as they journeyed east, and Ivan watched the dusky blue curves of snowhills rising in the twilight. Only two days before he had been brought before the area commissar, Maj. Andrei Dolotov from Simferopol. Dolotov's almond-shaped eyes had been gloomy as they viewed Ivan. He seemed a strangely passive and unhurried man for an officer in such high position, and he had had a withdrawn and secretive manner that gave his bulky body the appearance of a wall. His way of speaking was emotionless and hushed.

He had seemed mildly surprised that Ivan had been in the Red army for nearly two months and still had not adapted to army life. He had reviewed his records. Every effort had been made to rehabilitate Moiseyev, to give him opportunity to change his views, to reform politically, but he had refused to cooperate. His file contained complaints from Odessa, from the Polit-Ruk of Kerch, and from the officers and men of Moiseyev's own unit. There had been the problem of Moiseyev spreading his subversive ideas among the other men, so that they were becoming contaminated with his undesirable ideology. This was, of course, in direct violation of orders from the polit-officers. Dolotov was curious as to why Moiseyev would not obey.

His voice was so quiet Ivan was unsure he had finished speaking, and hesitated a moment. There was an oppressiveness in the room that made it hard to think. Ivan suddenly felt that he needed air. With a great effort he prayed briefly and took a breath. His head suddenly cleared as he addressed himself to Dolotov.

"Comrade commissar, the Bible teaches believers to obey the authorities placed over them. It is my deep desire to do this. But the Bible further teaches us that our supreme Master is God. His authority demands from us complete obedience and commitment. I beg of you to understand that I have two sets of loyalties—loyalty to the state and loyalty to God. If I am commanded to do something that would cause me to disobey God, then I am obliged to put my loyalty to Him first."

A dark flicker of change passed over the commissar's face; then he seemed to ponder an idea before he spoke.

"You are bound and shackled by these Baptist ideas. Very well—perhaps it would be helpful to you to experience the seriousness of your position if you had a taste of real prison. It is possible such a procedure will be more effective than all the reeducation programs in Kerch. Then we will see if you do not change your story."

Why the commissar had chosen such a far-flung place, Ivan could not guess. There were prisons close by on the Black Sea. Perhaps the ordeal of a long journey in the dead of winter was part of the strategy.

Ivan inhaled deeply. The air coming in the train door had somehow changed. It seemed heavier, with a chemical sharpness. Behind him in the car, there was a stirring. People began gathering their things more closely about them. An old man produced a rope from the inside of a lumpy blanket and began deftly tying the blanket into a bundle. A burly Cossack finished off the pan of melted snow that rocked on the floor in front of the small heater. An unshaven sergeant cursed as the train lurched suddenly. Two young soldiers, their eyes hard with anger, stood together. In the far distance, almost melting into the deep twilight, Ivan could see a forest of smokestacks pouring black clouds into the sky. Here and there tongues of orange flame seemed to lick the heavens.

The old man hunched behind Ivan at the door, peering out ahead of the train as far as he could see. " 'Sverdlovsk, the City on the Ridge.' " His words were spoken in the lifting, questioning accent of Odessa. " 'Worker and Warrior.' Well, I'm to be both there, and so are you, comrade." The guard, now roused from his dozing, pushed the old soldier roughly from the door and stationed himself beside Ivan without comment.

The engine began to brake. Shuddering, the train rattled and bumped over switches. The men crowded as close as they dared to the open door, straining to see the city, eager for the end of the tedium of the long journey. A pale star twinkled above a row of firs along the side of the track. Ivan watched its gentle light. His mind stirred, remembering a fragment of Scripture that his father loved: "And those who have insight will shine brightly like the brightness of the expanse of heaven, and those who lead the many to righteousness, like the stars forever and ever."

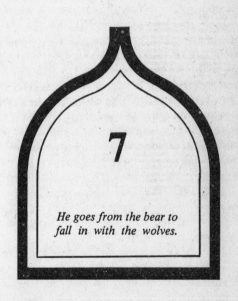

7

He goes from the bear to fall in with the wolves.

His cell was very small and cold and without light. When his eyes became accustomed to the dark he could make out a bunk along one wall and only enough space in the cell for him to fully extend his arm and touch the opposite side. The cell door had a small window near the top through which the guards shone flashlights during the night. His bones ached with inactivity. Painfully he pulled off his boots and pressed his stockinged feet against the damp cement wall. After the constant swaying of the train, the clatter of the wheels, and the hum of prisoners' voices, the cell was grave-like in its deathly stillness and silence. Ivan lay in the cold, his exhaustion unrelieved by sleep. The old man's words, "warrior and worker," turned in his mind like the wheels of the train. His mind moved to his experience on the heavenly planet with the angel. "You still have much work to do," the angel had said. *Warrior and worker.* Cold fear like a thin sheet of ice seemed to hang over his bunk close above him in the dark. What work was ahead? What warring? The fear, as if suspended by ropes, seemed to slip a notch closer to his face. "My soul waits in silence for God only; from Him is my salvation. He only is my rock and my salvation, my stronghold; I shall not be greatly shaken."

The interrogation room of the prison was in a frame building a few paces from Ivan's cellblock. It was a spacious room, with sagging wood floors and a painted radiator that ran the length of the room and reminded Ivan suddenly of his kindergarten on the collective farm in Moldavia. Some ferns at the end of the room decorated a few wooden steps leading to a very small platform on which was placed a picture of Lenin. Ivan guessed that the room was used also for cultural events.

An official of the prison sat behind a conference table

covered in purple cloth at the side of the room. Four other men in plain clothes sat at another table nearby. But it was the prison officer who spoke. In his hands were Ivan's documents.

It was commendable that Moiseyev had taken the oath of loyalty to the Red army. This was something Baptists often refused. Moiseyev had started off well, but had quickly proved to be an agitator, refusing correction, determined to cling to his old beliefs and to reject Soviet socialist teaching, seeking to persuade others to do the same. His loyalty to the Red army was under question, and his attitude toward authority ran afoul of all military life. In spite of dedicated efforts on the part of his superiors toward his reeducation, Moiseyev had spurned all such assistance and had created incident after incident in his desire to disrupt. It was an example of the clemency of the Soviet state that he was given so many opportunities to change his views. There was no question that already there was much evidence against him. Did he know that he could be brought to trial and sentenced to prison for seven years? Article 142 of the criminal code could be brought to bear since he had openly admitted he was a member of an unregistered Baptist group. There were articles 181 and 182 concerning bearing false witness. It had been established that much of his conversation was composed of utter, impossible lies, and that he had several times perjured himself. Article 190, paragraph one, was relevant. In his letter writing he had deliberately distributed literature containing false statements slandering the Soviet state and the Red army. His letters to his family had been copied and were positive proof. In the matter of article 58, paragraph 10, concerning anti-Soviet agitation, his situation was very serious indeed. Already he was inside the walls of a prison. Still, he was given yet another opportunity to avail himself of reeducation here in Sverdlovsk. If he refused to cooperate, persuasive measures would be administered.

Ivan spoke slowly, concentrating on his words as he formed them. It was often difficult not to be able to speak in his native

Moldavian. Russian constructions and endings would vanish from his memory when he was tired or most needed them.

"I have done nothing against the Soviet state. I have desired to quietly do my work in the army and at the same time worship and praise God. As for disturbances, it is the military who makes them, not I. As for staying here for seven years, I will, if it pleases God. If not, then tomorrow I shall be sent back to my base. Of this I am certain."

The new cell to which Ivan was sent was a tiny cubicle like a cage, four feet square. Taking up most of the floor space was a small bench similar to the ones small children use in schools. Like the first cell, it was very cold and without light. For two days Ivan painfully huddled on the stool, time wrapped around him like a dark cloth, torn only by the opening of the cell door for bread and weak coffee to be passed in and the waste bucket to be passed out.

Once or twice when awakening in a suffocating panic after a sleep, the sense of Christ's presence with Him was so tangible and quieting that Ivan wept with joy, the freezing agony in his cramped limbs dulled.

Hot pain shot through his muscles when he was finally pulled out of the cell and stood upright in the blazing light of the corridor. A guard jabbed him with the barrel of a machine gun, prodding him outside into the intense cold to the interrogation building. The same prison authority stood beside the table, his hand fingering a dog whip he had tucked into his belt.

"So you are out of your hole and breathing good socialist air! It seems you did not spend your time begging for release in the past two days; you have done some thinking, then. Perhaps you are willing now to take off the blindfold you have put over your own eyes and to enter the real Soviet world."

Ivan felt the rims of his eyes burning in the pale sunlight. He tried to control an irrational feeling that if he spoke his voice would be too faint to be heard. The official's face blazed before him. His words were slow in coming.

"There is a Scripture that says the lives of believers are hid with Christ in God. That is the real world and I am in it."

At Ivan's reply the officer stared speechless for a long minute. Grasping his whip he struck the conference table dramatically. He struck it again and again as if lashing a beast, his eyes never for a moment leaving Ivan's face.

As a child on the collective farm, Ivan had seen a drunken worker beat an ox. The animal, yoked and tied in a pen, had no escape. Blood had run down its legs and dripped in the mud from the flesh laid bare by the worker's whip. Some shift in Ivan's mind suddenly filled him with horror.

"This is the real world!" the officer was shouting, advancing to Ivan, the whip erect in his shaking hand. "You imagine that God can hide you from what is ahead for you? We will see how you feel when your God does not save you from the reality I will choose for you."

For a moment Ivan braced himself for the cut of the whip he expected. But the officer wheeled abruptly, his steps firing like bullets across the long room. In an instant two guards appeared, shoving Ivan ahead of them toward the prison.

Ivan hesitated in fear at the small door opened for him by the guard. "Inside, inside!" The guard heaved his rifle into Ivan's back, sending him skidding into the small cell. The door was instantly slammed and bolted. Water splashed over his boots and streamed down the walls. A dim light hung in a cage from the low ceiling, partially obscured by a crisscross of ice-covered pipes. Water dripped rapidly from every pipe, trickled from the seams, spurted from the connections, and drained sluggishly into a drain coated with ice in a corner of the cell. Almost immediately Ivan discovered it was not possible to stand anywhere out of the dripping, icy water. It showered his coat and ran down the back of his neck as he hunched into his clothing. An impulse to pound on the milky ice of the door seized him. Within minutes he began to shake violently. "Be gracious unto me, O God, be gracious unto me, for my soul takes refuge in Thee; and in the shadow of Thy wings I will take refuge, until destruction passes by. I will cry to God Most High, to God who accomplishes all things for me. He will send from heaven and save me." Through the ragged curtain of water he was startled by the unmoving eyes of a guard watching him from the door peephole. "Thou hast taken account of my wanderings; put my tears in Thy bottle; are they not in Thy book? Then my enemies will turn back in the day when I call; this I know, that God is for me."

By pressing himself into a corner of the cell, his back to the downfall, Ivan found he could avoid most of the water. Over and over he repeated the words of the psalm that seemed to come from beside him, from all around the cell. At the same time, his mind, independent in some way from the Scriptures he was half-shouting, was in a torment to escape.

As time passed the frenzied shaking of his body slowed into a terrible ache that began to spread from every joint in his body and to his back and head. His feet, pressed into his soaking boots, were in an agony of pain that forced him onto the floor of the cell. Half-kneeling in the ice and water, he began to imagine he was in an Orthodox cathedral with banks of candles flickering warmly on richly framed icons. Many people were worshiping all around and a glory of music and praise filled the cathedral. The service was long, very long.

This time the interrogation room was within the prison block itself, a large stone room with a smoky fire burning near a desk. Ivan lay on a cot at the far end of the room away from the fireplace, an electric heater glowing on the floor beside him. How he had been brought to the cot or how long ago, he had no idea. He was aware of the smell of singed cloth as he began to rouse. Stiffly he raised himself. A high, barred window, dry walls, a few prison officials around the fireplace came into view and then slid away as he fell back. A guard standing behind him yanked him violently to a sitting position, cursing the dead weight of Ivan's body.

It seemed unimportant what the officer was saying, but Ivan tried to listen. He felt terribly ill. " . . . You will receive your ration of bread and coffee. It is our determination to return you to your base at Kerch conformable to the standards for a Soviet youth. Those are our orders. You have proven to be obstinate, Moiseyev, but I think we have demonstrated to you that you are not going to have your way. As soon as you indicate your willingness to reform, we will consider that sufficient progress to discharge you from here and see that you are able to resume your training period as the military intends and as is your obligation to the Soviet Union."

A mug of weak coffee was placed on the table beside Ivan's cot, a thin tin plate of bread serving as an unsteady lid. Prayerfully Ivan lifted the cup to his lips, breathing in the steam of the coffee. Never had the symbolic wine of the Lord's Supper seemed as holy as this cup. Christ's words flooded his mind. "This is My blood of the covenant, which is to be shed on behalf of many." With a surge of love, Ivan drained the mug. Reverently he broke off a chunk of bread. "Take, eat; this is My body."

"We have some papers here, Moiseyev, which you might wish to sign," the officer continued. "They indicate your wiflingness to cooperate fully with Colonel Malsin, commander of your base in Kerch, and to give your complete obedience to any order that comes from any officer of any department for the duration of your service in the Red army. When you finish eating, your signature is all I need to begin the procedure for your release."

In the following days Ivan was even further plunged into the prison's nightmare world. "You are being sent to the 'room of the frozen,' " an old guard had whispered to him. "Give in! You won't live." How many hours *could* he live, Ivan wondered, in a refrigeration cell? Light snow covered the cells on the walls and ceiling as the thick door thudded shut. Time passed with his fear mounting. Pain began, and still the door remained sealed. The whiteness of the cell seemed luminous. Scriptures he knew, memories of home, and the knowledge of the light-filled place to which he was going finally quieted him. Gradually the fear and pain subsided and he began to doze. Profoundly thankful, he lay down on the floor of the cell .

At the beginning, he had thought the pressing and squeezing was a dream. He was a cosmonaut, drifting into freezing space. But the pressure suit was real and the shouts in his ears, "Will you give in? Will you change your beliefs?" jarred him into consciousness. He was strangling. He couldn't breathe. In space there were angels appearing and disappearing in their brilliance. "For He will give His angels charge concerning you, to guard you in all your ways." *If I explode, I shall explode into heaven.* The pressure was increased. Ivan tried to help the suit, tried himself to break through the anguish and suffocation to that lush place he had been with the angel. "Will you change your beliefs? We will stop the pressure. Change or you will be here seven years." He was not sure they could hear his voice. He gasped the words with tremendous effort. "If it is God's will, I will be here. If not . . . gone tomorrow . . . ."

The prison officer crumpled his empty Belomor package into the waste basket by his desk and fumbled through his drawer for more cigarettes. He lit one and inhaled with concentration. He had no further instructions on how to proceed. As a soldier Moiseyev ought to be charged and sentenced by a military tribunal. It was possible to keep him indefinitely at Sverdlovsk, of course, but he had no orders to that effect. Technically the prison committee had carried out its responsibility. For twelve days Moiseyev had been exposed to the most thorough of interrogations and reeducation techniques. Other than shipping him to Kerch in a box, there was no more to be done. Moiseyev would have a long uncomfortable train journey back to Kerch in which to recover and think over his future. Let the commissars in Kerch or Odessa worry about what to do with him. They could not complain that Sverdlovsk techniques had not been vigorously applied. Sverdlovsk would wash its hands of Moiseyev.

The officer's eye was caught by a small bird alighting on the smudged snow of his window sill. It pecked at the frozen crumbs he placed there day by day. There were fewer birds every year since all the new industry came in. He watched the bird anxiously. The sky was dirty. The snow was dirty. Everything was dirty these days.

8

*You shared your Bread
with me, and in the act
gave me back all Russia.*

The end of winter was unseasonably warm for Kerch. Lace circles of light snow still fell lazily in the early mornings, but the rigor of training eased a little in the milder temperatures. The Polit-Ruk had warned Ivan to say nothing about his assignment in Sverdlovsk—an order easy to obey since his every moment was engaged in a hectic program of catching up to his unit in military and political studies. In addition, he had been assigned as chauffeur to Colonel Malsin himself, with sudden and unpredictable calls for his services. Once in a while, when he was seated in class with the other soldiers, Ivan's sped-up world seemed to slow down and blend momentarily into a peaceful whole.

The horrors of Sverdlovsk were retold but once, in quiet murmurs over a chessboard to Sergei. The bishops and pawns and knights never moved more erratically as Ivan and his friend sat in an obscure corner of the common room. Verses of Scripture and phrases of encouragement floated back and forth almost imperceptibly under the swells of laughter and banter that rolled over the room.

As spring came, Ivan began to notice a wonderful thing happening. Even on days when a time of prayer was impossible, increasingly he was experiencing an almost overwhelming sense of the presence of God. Love blazed like an icon candle inside him. He was astonished that no blast of injustice from outside caused it to flicker. Even tonight, hurrying to the evening lecture on scientific atheism, he felt no impatience. He was tired; his muscles ached. But praise to God welled up in his heart.

There had been no need for haste. The soldiers were clustered around a glowing heater in the front of the classroom, joking as they faced the red electric coils. Ivan sat down and rested his head on the arm of his desk. His bunkmate, Vladimir Albu, noticed him and was not surprised that he could sleep, even in such clamor. The wall clock showed several minutes after the hour. The instructor was still missing from the room.

The men began diffidently to take their seats, unwilling to leave the comfort of the heater, yet uneasy at being found in the wrong place if an officer suddenly arrived after all. But the time wore on. Suddenly Vladimir had an idea. "Let's have our own lecture! Let's have a political debate."

Interest stirred slightly. That would be one way of passing the time. No one dared to leave the classroom without an order.

"Our comrade, Ivan Vasilievich, has sometimes taken a stand against the theories of this class. Yet we have not heard his position fully articulated. We shall debate the question: What is the difference between Ivan's God and our god (which he claims is the state)?"

Ivan had been praying before the class began. Now, with an inward lift he agreed to the debate. Some of the men pulled out their cigarettes and twisted toward him in their chairs. There was an intensity in the classroom.

Vladimir started it off. "All right, Ivan, who is your God?"

Ivan's pleasure at what looked like an opportunity to preach to the class was short-lived. "My God," he began, "is almighty and all-powerful—."

In the middle of the room a sergeant from Armenia coughed on his cigarette and stamped impatiently on the floor. He groaned in exasperation. "Just a minute, Moiseyev. Your God is *all-powerful?*"

"Yes."

"He can do anything?"

"Yes."

The sudden challenge in the sergeant's eyes was unmistakable. The soldiers stared in enjoyment.

"If your God is all-powerful and can do anything, prove it!"

Murmurs of assent came from all corners of the room. Ivan's life had awakened disturbing questions in many minds. The sergeant spoke loudly. "If your God can do anything, let Him get me a leave tomorrow to go home. Then I'll believe in Him!"

"Fair enough!" Vladimir exclaimed. Here would be something scientific. Black and white. Yes or no. Leaves were rare. There would be nothing inconclusive and mysterious about a contest like this.

Responses to the challenge came quickly.

"Yes, Ivan Vasilievich. I've listened to you! Up to now, everything you've said sounds like fairy tales. But if your God gives Pyotr Alexandrovich Prokhorov a leave, then we'll believe there is a God in the sky."

"Right! If your God does it, we will believe that He is a living God and can do everything!"

"Most certainly. Let your God prove Himself! Then even we will believe."

Gazing at the excited men, Ivan prayed fervently in his spirit. The soldiers waited, gradually sobered by the earnest struggle they could see in Ivan's face.

Lord! Can this be from You? Will You be tempted by men? What they ask, is this right, Lord?

"Come on, Ivan Vasilievich! Let's prove your living God!" The sergeant shifted uneasily in his chair. Somehow the challenge was being taken too seriously.

Suddenly Ivan thought of the Old Testament contest between the prophets of Baal and Elijah. With a new inward quietness he asked again for direction. Unmistakably the words came into his consciousness: "Tell them I will do this."

Every eye in the room stared as Ivan answered. His voice had an assurance that astonished the men. Turning to the sergeant he spoke clearly enough for every person to easily hear his reply. "Tomorrow the Lord says you will go home on leave. Now, you must do what I tell you. Throw away your cigarette." The sergeant obeyed. "And now pull the pack out of your pocket."

With an elaborate shrug Prokhorov produced his pack of cigarettes. Pulling himself up from his desk he walked slowly to the heater and dropped the pack behind the red-hot grate. In a moment it flared up and burned brightly.

For the first time Ivan noticed that a large crowd of soldiers had gathered at the two side doors of the lecture room, spilling over into a line around the walls of the room. A stillness like an invisible mist seemed to hang in the air. Finally the spell was broken by the arrival of several breathless officers. The evening's class began.

It wasn't until after taps that Ivan was able to speak again with the sergeant. He found him lying sleepless on his bunk, staring at the sprinkle of stars he could see from the window nearby. The assurance of Ivan's reply had unnerved him. He had been able to think of nothing else all evening. It was absurdity, but over and over he found himself in a state of excitement. He half-believed that something might happen in the morning!

"There is much to talk to you about, comrade." Ivan's voice was a whisper. Prokhorov raised himself on one elbow, pulling his blanket over his shoulder.

"Why aren't you asleep, Moiseyev?"

Ivan smiled. "Because there is much to talk to you about. Since you will become a believer tomorrow, there are many things I must tell you."

"You're crazy, Moiseyev. Why don't you go back to bed? And you're going to get cold."

Pyotr Prokhorov squinted nervously at Ivan in the dark. The story of Moiseyev standing all night in below-zero December weather flashed into his mind. He was reassured to see that Ivan carried his blanket with him and swept it around himself as he huddled on the end of Prokhorov's bunk.

"You said you would believe if God gives you a leave tomorrow morning?"

"Of course. Many of us said we would believe."

"But it is for you, Pyotr Alexandrovich, that God is going to do this miracle. I must tell you what the Bible teaches."

In spite of a feeling of uneasiness, Prokhorov's interest was captured by the things Moiseyev said. Never before had he heard such ideas spoken with such absolute conviction. The teachings of the Bible were a world away from the strange icons he had seen in museums or the bizarre stories he had been told about the Christian Scriptures. Was it possible that the emptiness in himself he had long ago accepted as part of the human condition was a longing for God as Moiseyev said? If God exists!

"Is there a prayer house in your city?"

The sergeant was amused. "You mean for the old ladies? Anyway, I do not think so."

"It is not only old ladies who go. Many men. Many young people. They will be able to help you. I can find out for you some names of believers in your city, but it will take time. The brethren in Kerch will know."

"There are people that believe like you do, in Kerch? And in my own city?"

Ivan grinned suddenly. "Of course! And you are going to minister joy to them when you tell them what the Lord has done. What praises they will raise! How they will welcome you!"

Prokhorov felt intensely uncomfortable.

"In the meetings of believers there will be some who have Bibles. At least one of the pastors will have a Bible. Probably most. Someone sometime will lend you Scriptures to read and they will suggest where to begin. I am sorry I have no Bible to lend you. For the moment you will have to believe what I say is true. I want to tell you all I can of what the Bible says. We must discuss the world and man and sin and God's plan for man's salvation."

The night wore on as the whispered monologue became a discussion. Two hours before reveille, Prokhorov stood and stretched quietly as Ivan ended a prayer. "Moiseyev, my head is so full of ideas, I may never sleep again. But thank you, comrade. Morning comes."

At the sound of the bugle, Ivan awoke immediately with a thrill of expectation. This would be a wonderful day. For once he was eager for the morning ordeal of long-distance running. Perhaps he might find Sergei and be able to tell him about Prokhorov and what the Lord had promised to do. But unexpectedly, there was to be no morning drill for Ivan.

The night delivery of bread had not been made. Ivan would leave for Kerch and pick up the bread supply that would be needed for breakfast. Ivan climbed into the cab of the small truck, singing as he turned the key in the ignition.

When he pulled back into the base almost an hour later, he was surprised at a small commotion near the garages where the trucks were parked. Curiously he jumped down from the truck and ran toward the crowd of soldiers milling about the gate. They were men from his own unit.

Excited shouting split the air.

"Ivan Vasilievich! Comrade Prokhorov has left on leave! Prokhorov has gone! We have been waiting to tell you!"

The soldiers were gathering around Ivan eagerly.

A general or a colonel had called their base from headquarters in Odessa with the order that Prokhorov be given immediate leave to go home. He had departed ten minutes after the phone call, running and leaping like a crazy man, jumping on the back of a mail truck that was leaving for the train.

Vladimir pushed to the front of the crowd and grabbed Ivan's arm. "The officers came out when they saw us all laughing and cheering. We told them what happened last night at the political lecture. You should have seen their faces when we said everything had turned out as you said, Vanya! Major Gidenko came out to see what was going on and when he heard the story, he sent some soldiers off to the train to bring Prokhorov back again. They left in a spray of melting snow, skidding all the way to the front gates. They arrived at the train station to see the very end of the train disappearing in the distance. Prokhorov was gone!"

Major Gidenko had only a moment of impatience as he watched the scene of Moiseyev's return to the base through binoculars from his office window. Good thing he had ordered Moiseyev brought immediately to him. With satisfaction he observed Ivan being pulled away from the excited group and the soldiers dispersed to their work. Gidenko had assumed that after Sverdlovsk, Moiseyev would settle down. He had sent a communique to Commissar Dolotov in Simferopol with assurances that the matter was in hand. Yet here was another disruption. Moiseyev was achieving a kind of fame in his unit. He was popular and a good soldier, and the men were interested in him and in his Baptist views. It was impossible to train a unit for military and political effectiveness with continuing incidents. There was something altogether unexplained about Moiseyev. Colonel Malsin, acting for Commissar Dolotov, had suggested Gidenko get to the bottom of it or arrange a transfer for Moiseyev to another unit where he was not known.

There was more involved in this present situation than met the eye. Moiseyev must have had contacts in Odessa to have known about Prokhorov's leave. Gidenko felt depressed. These difficulties were time-consuming and involved an uncomfortable number of men. He had lost confidence that the Moiseyev problem would be easily resolved. The question of Prokhorov was another matter. He had always been politically sound. Some troublemaker had invented the story that Prokhorov had declared himself to be a believer. That could be cleared up when Prokhorov returned.

It was too bad that Colonel Malsin had decided to become involved. There were enough leaders in the Polit-Ruk to handle ten Moiseyevs. But Malsin was particularly sensitive about religious matters. Gidenko rose and saluted as Malsin's small figure came into the room. Unfortunate that Malsin wouldn't leave these matters to others.

"If it weren't for his popularity with the men, *I* could have him taken care of." Malsin's sharp voice pointed accusingly at Gidenko. "He's an excellent chauffeur—believe me, I watch him carefully. Always on time, car in perfect condition, always sober, always correct in every way. He's even earned merit points from various officers. Merit points, and he's only been in six or seven months!"

A long time, Gidenko thought, for a young man to defy the authority of the Red army. It was difficult to explain.

"I've seen how Baptists operate before this. They're stubborn and underhanded," Malsin continued, "and they're secretive. But they make sure they have good work records. They know more about the laws of our country—or think they do—more than all you political lawyers put together."

"Technically, according to the law, Moiseyev has committed no criminal act," Gidenko responded. "No doubt he is aware of that." Gidenko opened the window of his office to let in some fresh sea air. Spring was a beautiful season in Kerch—it came early and stayed late. He took a deep breath and wished Moiseyev would arrive.

"Nonsense! You'll have me questioning your competence, Gidenko. I could have Moiseyev arrested this minute as an agitator. For one thing, there are laws, I believe, against anti-Soviet activity and the propagation of religion. Moiseyev is guilty of both. And as far as that goes, there are those occasions, as you very well know, where some laws must be set aside and one is called upon to act 'administratively.' "

Gidenko disliked having to debate the colonel. "Unfortunately, Moiseyev cannot be dealt with quietly. He has become the center of attention. The men in his unit must not misinterpret our actions as antireligious, colonel. And as for his actions being anti-Soviet, that is clear to us, of course. It may not be so clear to the men. It is not altogether a simple problem."

Malsin frowned irritably at Gidenko as he lit a cigarette. The case had not been handled correctly from the beginning. Five days without food! A few hours in the snow! Time enough for him to fantasize a story about angels, that was all. And now another incident again with Moiseyev and his God in the leading role. Malsin's tense face was momentarily lit in the dim room by the flare of his match.

"There is a scientific explanation for Prokhorov's leave, if we can procure the facts. There are no mysteries in this world. There is only ignorance."

There was a brief knock as Ivan was escorted into the room. The door shut hastily.

Malsin inhaled deeply. The boy was handsome enough, with chiseled features and clear, steady eyes. His expression was attentive but set in a way Malsin did not like.

"Moiseyev, I'll come straight to the point. I am Colonel Malsin, the supreme commander of this entire base. I have reason to suspect you of subversive, anti-Soviet activity. In order to have known about the order which arrived at our base only this morning for a leave for Sgt. Pyotr Alexandrovich Prokhorov you would have had to work through accomplices in Odessa."

Gidenko turned in his chair and gazed impassively out of the window. Four stories below and in front of his building, he could see passing soldiers glancing up from time to time. So word had been passed already that Moiseyev was being questioned once more.

"It has been established that you have been attempting to draw into your religious fantasies as many soldiers as possible who do not have a strong materialistic and socialist view of life. You have been trying in every way to tear them away from productive activities and active communist creative training and labor. As your commander I order you to desist immediately from all such activities and to fully confess your subversive activities."

The major swiveled slowly to face back into the room. Moiseyev had not flinched. He said nothing.

"First of all," Malsin continued in an even more brittle voice, "how did you learn of Prokhorov's impending leave? There was absolutely no advance notice of it at Kerch. I require a complete explanation."

Ivan's voice was steady and distinct. "Comrade colonel, I did not know that Sergeant Prokhorov would be granted a leave. God told me He would give him leave to demonstrate His existence. And God did."

Malsin flushed furiously. More distinctly, as if he had not heard, he repeated his question.

Gidenko wished he had had a drink. This was going to take a long time.

The morning dragged into the early afternoon, punctuated by fury and threats, elaborate intricate questionings on tracks familiar to Gidenko. Malsin's energy seemed enormous, yet Moiseyev answered quietly, sometimes waiting so long with his answers that Gidenko wondered if he were ill. Surely without breakfast and dinner the boy would wear down. Gidenko wished he would: the session seemed endless. And he could have handled it better himself.

Suddenly Malsin's deathly voice excused Moiseyev to his unit. As the door closed behind him Malsin spoke through clenched teeth. His face was white with anger. "And he eats Soviet bread!" he said.

9

The poor sing;
the rich listen.

Uncertainty had hung in the air all summer. Ivan had heard a rumor that he was to be sent away to another unit. He knew Malsin was determined to get rid of him. But the fragrant seaport spring gave way to the glories of summer and early autumn, and still he remained in Kerch, propelled through the hot days and nights by a schedule that left no time for speculation. He tried to excel in everything: political classes, target practice, calisthenics, advanced mechanics, his hours of chauffeuring, night drills, field maneuvers. Each was an opportunity to bring glory to God.

But late this afternoon something more of the transfer had leaked out. He had been hurrying to the base post office before a class to mail a letter home when he heard his name raised in a small crowd of soldiers standing at the door of the officers' dining hall.

"What has Moiseyev *done*?" Vladimir Yakovlevich was demanding. "Is it not true that our Constitution guarantees freedom of conscience to anyone? Is it against the law to be a believer? What law does he break that he is so frequently questioned?"

Ivan could not hear the officer's reply or the curt response of the polit-officer.

A husky Ukrainian edged closer to the center of the group. "Why is he to be sent away? What has he done to be transferred out of our unit?" The officer began to answer again, but his reply was lost to Ivan as he pushed open the heavy door of the post office. His hand was unsteady as he sorted out the small kopecks for a stamp. Any incident was excuse enough for the political leader to initiate another series of interrogations.

Colonel Malsin or Major Gidenko would be infuriated if informed that the men were defending Ivan.

Several sets of tire tracks led down the road toward the lecture hall. They had been made earlier by the small pickup truck that delivered wood for the kitchen ovens. Dust lay in the ruts and covered his boots as he walked. All over the world, he supposed, there were men and women who lived freely as Christians and bore witness to Jesus Christ. His eyes scanned the lush fields in the distance. They used to call this "Holy Russia," he was thinking. But no more.

A few leaves spun in the evening air, rocking to the ground in splashes of gold. As uncertain as his days were, the Lord was certain. His help would never fail. *Praise, praise, praise to God most high. Most holy, most worthy, most wonderful, mighty God. Prince of Peace.* He lifted his face in joy toward the evening sky. Flames of fire lit the heavens so brightly that the few early stars faded instantly in the glow.

Ivan leaned in terror against the trunk of a tree in a small grove on the corner of the road. The sky seemed to be pouring flame, yet the torrents of fire came no closer to the earth. Waves of warmth and sweetness melted his fear as he stared transfixed at the sky. Gradually letters appeared in the midst of the flames. So overwhelming was the spectacle that Ivan gazed uncomprehending at the scene. There was an inner urging. *Read!*

Like a child learning to spell he gazed at each individual letter. Slowly the message sank into his mind. *Ya pridu skoro* ("I will come soon"). The words were alive in some incomprehensible way. They seemed to leap with a joy that grew in Ivan's heart. Over and over the words repeated themselves in a dance of celebration.

With a rush of despair Ivan realized that the vision was disappearing. The flames fell back into the darkness of the sky. Suddenly they were gone. Perhaps it was only a moment that he stood there before a passing classmate pulled his arm.

"Come on, Moiseyev. This is no time to daydream. We'll be late for our lecture."

Blindly Ivan fell in beside him. A sense that his heart was breaking made it impossible for him to speak. His companion was chatting as they walked. Ivan tried to concentrate, to nod, to enter the hall normally, to take his seat composed. Like the others he took notes, trying to keep up with the instructor's rapid delivery. At the end of the lecture, like the others he snapped his briefcase shut and hurried to the next class, the evening drill, to the barracks, to bed. When the battle alarm was sounded in the middle of the sultry night, he was still awake, caught up in a joy and longing that made sleep impossible. Through the drill, through the second drill that came on the heels of the first, through the remaining hours of the night, he lay praying and wishing the angel on the planet had not told him he still had much work to do on earth.

The first light of morning that pulled Ivan out of bed still praising God, fell irritably on Colonel Malsin. He coughed wearily as he tried to sit up in bed and remember why this was an unpleasant day. In the apartment kitchen, he could hear his wife preparing breakfast and talking softly to their young son. The smell of fish hung on the air. He could hear the water being poured into the samovar for tea.

Ah! Today Unit 61968T was being assigned to the harvest detail at Zhostena. Moiseyev's unit. Malsin didn't like unfinished business. The problem with Moiseyev was that he had succeeded in winning so many friends in the unit. It wasn't hard to understand. He was personable enough, worked hard, helped anybody. Of course it was a technique to spread his teachings. But Gidenko was right. Legally he had done nothing wrong. And he was clever enough to attract all the attention he could.

Malsin stirred his glass of tea. His wife, Galina, watched him pensively.

"It's bad business," he finally said, "letting Moiseyev go off

96

with his unit to the harvesting. I should have transferred him to another unit where he isn't known. Steps could have been taken privately and quickly."

"It makes me nervous. All these strange stories about the boy. You say they have scientific explanations, but . . . ." Her voice trailed off and she turned her eyes to gaze at the brightening morning sky.

Malsin swallowed his tea so quickly he burned his tongue. "What are you saying, Lena? You of all people, a Soviet teacher, and you doubt that science can explain everything? That's very strange. I understood it is your very task to educate the young students in the spirit of Marxist-Leninism."

Impulsively his wife leaned across the table toward him. Her slightly graying hair was bleached in the modern way and a yellow strand fell across her cheek. Her wide-set blue eyes looked suddenly playful. "Volodia, don't be stuffy with me. Doesn't all this scientific materialism sometimes *bore* you? Surely it must."

Malsin threw a look over his shoulder at their son dressing in the bedroom as his wife continued.

"Don't you ever marvel that some of the best people in our country—the hardest-working, the most honest—are Moiseyev's Baptists?"

"What I wonder is how a woman of your education and position can speak this way!" Malsin became suddenly infuriated at the restless sigh his wife didn't bother to stifle. His voice quickened. "The very idea of God is a catchall explanation for natural phenomena that is as yet not understood. Or what is worse, *God* is simply a word that has been used in our country's history for centuries to confirm injustice and support cruelty and hypocrisy. These things you know very well."

His burned tongue would be sore all day. Jamming his papers into his briefcase he ignored the plate of fish his wife placed on the table. "This cancer of religion must be cut out of our society if communism is to fully triumph. How can all

97

citizens advance into the twenty-first century if some are still shackled to religious prejudices that have not been overcome? Where is the New Soviet Man then?"

Galina hesitated before she spoke. "But Volodia, we are told that the struggle against religion requires ideological weapons alone, since compulsory tactics increase religious fervor. You aren't thinking of compulsory tactics for young Moiseyev?" A memory troubled her face.

Malsin's voice was impatient. "When I need to answer to a schoolteacher for my military or political tactics I will join the line of ten-year-olds at your desk." It was a credit to him, he felt, that he would not slam the door.

The weeks in the harvest fields, living in tents and under the vast Ukrainian sky passed far too quickly for Ivan. Many of the others, especially soldiers from the cities, had grown tired of the drudgery of harvest and the bleakness of the bare countryside. The agricultural workers on the state farm, with their simple speech and muddy hands, were uninteresting to them, and in the evenings they yawned restlessly in the tents, reading or playing chess and hoping that the harvest would soon be in.

But for Ivan, it was home. Not that the collective on which his parents worked was as large as this one, nor was the harvest similar. But the feel of the hazy afternoon sun on his back, the smell of the earth, the sound of voices calling back and forth in the open air sometimes made him forget where he was, and he would straighten his back, expecting some of his brothers or his mother to be working nearby.

It had been a good time of rest and spiritual refreshment, over too soon, Ivan thought. He sat watching the the tow truck ahead of him as it pulled his own Zil-164 with its disabled driveshaft. The convoy of army trucks filled with earth and returning soldiers snaked over the rolling hills of the evening countryside toward Kerch.

Suddenly the peacefulness of Ivan's thoughts was dispelled

by a loud banging under the truck. He honked for the attention of Fyodor Tarusov in the tow truck. They were approaching the top of a hill. Fyodor eased the tandem to the side of the road and jumped out, along with Alexi Kuprin.

"The universal joint?" Alexi guessed.

Ivan nodded, hopping out into the cold evening countryside. "Give me the flashlight and repair kit. I'll just disconnect it. Put the emergency brake on, will you?"

A dog howled somewhere in the distance. An owl hooted. It was a starless night. Fyodor glanced at his watch with a groan. "Ten o'clock at night. We'll never get any sleep."

Even in the poor light of the flashlight Ivan could see it was the universal joint. With a grunt of effort in the small space he finally scooted his body under it. He rummaged in his kit for a wrench, then managed to take the joint apart. The instant he felt the shift of the truck he knew Alexi had not put on the emergency brake. With a lunge he tried to roll out from under the truck as it moved forward. He let out a desperate shout: "Reverse!"

The strange thing in the next few minutes of pain was that he was aware of everything. The rear wheel crushing into his shoulder and chest, the horror on Fyodor's face, the churning of the engine as Alexi tried repeatedly to get the tow truck to reverse. The smell of tire rubber and oil filled his nostrils in the intense dark under the truck. From the corner of his eye he could see the flashlight where it had rolled onto the road. In the tiny spot of its light small insects began to fly. Pain was ripping through his chest, strangling his breath. He was perfectly aware that Alexi couldn't get the truck into reverse. Surely soon he would be with the angel. "Jesus." "Jesus."

With a slight jolt, the engine roared and the six pairs of wheels rolled back. Ivan pulled himself away from the truck and collapsed onto his mangled arm and chest in the road.

When he opened his eyes, a hot sheet of pain seemed to be burning into him. A small group of doctors beside his bed came into focus and beyond them a white wall and a narrow window curtained in sagging white cotton. He tried to speak, but his mouth was crusted with fever.

One of the doctors bent over him with interest, reading the question in his eyes. Her voice was kind. "You have been transferred to Simferopol Military Hospital, Ivan Vasilievich." Her expression remained unchanged as she pulled the thermometer from under his arm.

A nurse began bathing his face in cool water. He tried to suck the moisture from the cloth as it touched his lips. Smiling, she held a glass for him to drink. The slightest move seemed to fling open floodgates of pain. The shallowest breathing took enormous effort. His eyes followed her hand as the nurse set the glass down on a small table beside his bed. His right arm was lying outside the covers. He stared at it in astonishment. The whole hand and wrist and the part of the arm he could see not covered by a sling was a dusky gray. It seemed unattached to his body. It was impossible for him to will the smallest movement in the swollen fingers. With his left hand he reached through the pain and touched the right wrist and back of the hand; it was ice cold. The rest of his body was fiery hot.

With the nurse raising him to a half-sitting position he thirstily gulped more water. He could see he was in a large ward. Some of the patients appeared very ill with dripping bottles and tubes and whirring machines attached to them. Some slept. Others were convalescing, stooping like old men from bed to chair or cautiously sitting up reading. A few watched Ivan intently.

The nurse moved away, carrying her basin and cloth with her. Ivan closed his eyes and began to pray.

By the time of the evening meal a surgeon came to tell Ivan that surgery was scheduled in the morning. A specialist had been sent for to perform the operation. His right arm that was so frighteningly cold was to be amputated. Part of his crushed lung would be removed.

Ivan watched the doctor leave the ward, stopping at occasional bedsides as he wearily made his way to the corridor. His white coat moved from one patient to another, pausing, nodding briefly, the back of his shoulders stooped in fatigue. When he had gone, the patients sank back into their private struggles with depression or pain or loneliness. A desperate rejection of the surgeon's words swept through Ivan's mind. His heart pounded against his injured lung. He began to be horrified at the thought of his body without an arm. "Hear my prayer, O Lord! And let my cry for help come to Thee. Do not hide Thy face from me in the day of my distress; incline Thine ear to me; in the day when I call answer me quickly."

Somehow Ivan had to get out of bed. He felt himself falling into a grief from which he could neither pray nor hope. In a rush of anguish he heaved himself to the edge of the bed and threw his legs over the side. He staggered wildly for balance as pain blackened the room. Desperation gave him breath.

Every eye in the room was fixed upon him in fear and astonishment.

"I cry aloud with my voice to the Lord; I make supplication with my voice to the Lord. I pour out my complaint before Him; I declare my trouble before Him. When my spirit was overwhelmed within me, Thou didst know my path. I cried out to Thee, O Lord; I said, Thou art my refuge, my portion in the land of the living. Give heed to my cry, for I am brought very low."

A passing nurse stopped in the doorway and entered the room slowly.

"Bring my soul out of prison, so that I may give thanks to Thy name; for Thou wilt deal bountifully with me."

Guiding Ivan with her hand under his left elbow, the nurse moved him into bed.

A great joy seemed to shake his body. Ivan smiled suddenly. "Thou *wilt* deal bountifully with me."

He remembered the nurse wiping his face with a wet cloth as he sank into a blessed darkness.

It was six o'clock in the morning when he awoke. For several moments Ivan lay motionless, trying to hold onto the sweet lightness of a dream. Gradually he became aware that he was lying on his back instead of hunched on his uninjured left side. His breathing was quiet. Cautiously he took a deep breath. His arms were folded above his head and he was able to gaze at the ward still wrapped in sleep. Quietly he began to give praise to the Lord for the enormous relief of this dream. He brought his right arm down carefully from behind his head to his side. It was perfectly whole, the fingernails pink, the flesh still slightly tanned from his work in the harvest fields. With both hands he raised himself to a sitting position and got out of bed. Smiling in wonder at the reality of the dream, he lightly punched his pillow and patted the side of the bed. He waved one arm above his head playfully, then the other. With his hands on his waist, he did a few deep bends.

In a supreme happiness he knelt in prayer at the end of his bed. Softly he whispered praises. "Praise the Lord. Praise the Lord, O my soul. I will praise the Lord while I live. I will sing praises to my God while I have my being. The Lord opens the eyes of the blind; the Lord raises up those who are bowed down; the Lord loves the righteous. Praise the Lord."

Eventually the man in the bed beside him began to moan. Someone on the other side of the ward was struggling to reach a glass of water. Daylight streaked the slate-colored sky in the window.

The lifelikeness of the dream amused Ivan. With a sleepy sigh he crawled into bed. He imagined himself floating into a delicious sleep.

The day nurse reached mechanically for the thermometer in the drawer of Ivan's table. He opened his eyes and gazed sleepily at her. The thermometer remained suspended in air as she stared fearfully at him. In an instant she was gone.

Rapid footsteps in the ward roused him a second time. The surgeon was standing beside the nurse. Some other doctors were hurrying into the room. Everyone appeared startled.

Ivan sat up defensively. What was happening? Suddenly a glory rolled over him. He had sat up! He stared at his hands in front of him. The sling lay on the top of his covers at the bottom of his bed. He began breathing deeply, entranced. He rubbed his hands together, then separated them in wonder.

The doctor was frightened. He groped for words. The nurse backed slightly away from the bed.

Finally, in a shaking voice, the doctor spoke: "Shall I take your temperature, Comrade Moiseyev?" Ivan flushed with happiness. "Of course I don't need my temperature taken, comrade doctor."

The surgeon continued to stare. Finally he put the medicine on the table. Hesitantly, his fingers probed Ivan's right hand. Gently lifting the sleeve of the hospital gown he glanced at the arm, his eyes returning again and again to the radiance of Ivan's face.

"I saw that you could not heal me." Ivan noticed that the nurse's face was white and that she had been joined by a small crowd of astonished employees. "And I turned to my heavenly Doctor, who healed me last night.

"Look!" With a grin, Ivan pulled back the blanket and stood on the floor. "Last night I was very ill. My temperature was high."

The nurse began to tremble as she nodded.

"Now I shall show you what my God can do." Ivan handed the thermometer to the doctor, who shook it down and placed it under Ivan's tongue. Some of the patients in the ward were gathering about the bottom of the bed. Others were calling softly from bed to bed, trying to discover and report what was going on.

The doctor removed the thermometer. "The temperature is normal, Moiseyev. Obviously. However, please return to your bed."

It was difficult for Ivan to comply. He wanted to jump, to shout, to fill the ward with the praises of God. When the small group of staff had finally gone, he raised himself on his elbow and began telling the electrified ward what God had done while he slept.

10

*What is taken in
with the milk
only goes out with the soul.*

Lieutenant Colonel Malsin slammed his report book on his desk. Never before had he had such an infuriating telephone call. The surgeon-general at Simferopol was an incompetent idiot. Yesterday he reported that major surgery was to be done on Ivan Moiseyev. Well and good. Let them amputate if they could not save his arm. Moiseyev would be away from his unit a very long time. Of course he understood that. His condition was critical. Certainly it was critical. The matter was settled. Malsin admitted to himself he had been relieved not to have Moiseyev back in Kerch. It seemed that fate had done his work for him. Moiseyev would be handicapped, perhaps discharged from the army. At any rate he would not be Kerch's problem any longer.

And today the surgeon-general telephones a preposterous story. There will be no surgery. Several surgeons have examined Ivan Moiseyev and he is miraculously healed. A man of science sputtering about miracles! This critically ill patient of yesterday has already been discharged and is on a bus returning to his unit. A man of science! Malsin would see that he was reported. Obviously he is unstable and incapable. Certainly Malsin would recommend examination by a psychiatrist.

His voice had trembled on the telephone. Malsin tried to disregard the ring of sincerity in his words. "Colonel, for the first time in my life I see that there really is a God. He healed Moiseyev! His condition is perfect. Even with months of work, I could have done nothing like that!"

It was disgusting to try to hide incompetence. If there had been a gross error in diagnosis, far better to admit it and take the consequences. With grim satisfaction, Malsin wrote out the report of Moiseyev's medical discharge. Every word the army surgeon had said about miracles and God would be sent to Moscow. Ringing the bell on his desk, he summoned the clerk to type the report.

Malsin took a deep breath as he poured his vodka. The Polit-Ruk would be ready for Moiseyev when he returned.

Much of the journey back to Kerch, Ivan sat praying and praising God in his spirit, watching the late November countryside spin by in a haze of frosty gray. It would snow any day. Agricultural workers, deep in the fields, gave a comradely salute as the bus rolled by. Small villages like his at home seemed to huddle into the cold earth for warmth. Small children, fat in their warm clothes, stood beside frozen puddles pondering the mystery of the bus as their babushkas stooped patiently to whisper in their ears. He loved it all: the people, the vast sky, the fields as far as he could see, the workers lashing the last crates of cabbages to the trucks. For a time he forgot his struggles and sat tall against the window, proud to be part of the great stream of life that was the Soviet Union.

"I have often had it happen," he had once written to his parents, "that after a mighty manifestation of God's power over me, Satan rages and tries as best he can to do evil." Now, short hours away from Kerch, he tried to prepare his heart for what might be ahead at the base. But the suddenness and viciousness of the attacks from the moment of his return shocked him.

Commissar Dolotov, from his Crimean headquarters, had given out the order: "Moiseyev must be broken." The head of the Kerch Polit-Ruk and the head of the military would answer to him for Moiseyev. Already one year of Moiseyev's service had passed and still he was an open believer. There were to be no further incidents and no problems from the men in his unit. Mismanage this case and both Gidenko and Malsin were finished.

Ivan had no sooner unpacked than he was called first to one polit-officer, then to another. He was investigated, questioned, lectured, threatened. He was summoned out of classes, during meals, often in the middle of the night.

It was known that in civilian life he had taken part in illegal activities in an unregistered church. That he was engaged in subversive work in the army was a known fact. How many Soviet soldiers had he already drawn into the whirlpool of his fantasies, torn away from constructive activities to secret conversations and activities? He could be sentenced at any time to seven years or more in a corrective labor camp for anti-Soviet agitation according to article 58, paragraph 10, of the criminal code. He was indifferent to the demands of his army work. He frequently seemed to be absent from classes and drills. There were sheets of complaints against him from his superior officers. He was insubordinate. The KGB was making inquiries about him. It would be necessary for him to have a psychiatric examination, a medical examination, a political examination. If there is a God, why is it that no one believes in Him? Can he quote the statements of Marx, Engels, and Lenin concerning God? Is it possible that he is deaf?

The shouting could continue for hours. Ivan tried not to listen. It was unnecessary because the questions were most often rhetorical. When answers were required they were repeated so forcibly, often with a blow to the back or head "to wake him up," that a long interval could pass in which Ivan could concentrate on prayer.

"What is the matter that you are withdrawn—you do not take part in cultural activities? Why is it men on the base, men not from your unit, sometimes come to ask you questions? Who are these men? Do you admit that you try to convert others to religion? Do you understand that such activity is prohibited by law? Your continuing disobedience is understood as a mad desire for suicide. Even your own religion disapproves of suicide . . . . You are in a religious delirium with your talk of angels and healings. Is it not true that such things are utterly against the philosophy of Lenin's scientific communism? Is not what you say about the meaninglessness of life without God simply a disintegration of the consciousness? What friends do you have in Odessa? When have you been in Odessa? There are inconsistencies in hundreds of your answers. Do you not have a commandment not to lie? What about your loyalty to the Soviet state? Have you not broken your army oath of loyalty? Why is it that we atheists deceive no one but you believers deceive the state with secret meetings and illegal publications? You are out of harmony with society . . . .

"It is only potential enemies who deny Marxist philosophy. You cannot be considered a Soviet citizen. You have joined yourself to corrupt people against whom the state must struggle and fight. We are building communism in the army more than in any other segment of Soviet life. How can you insist you are a loyal soldier and yet by your beliefs seek to undermine the scientific philosophical system of the army and our socialist states?"

There were hours when Malsin himself joined Gidenko's interrogations. At such times he would conduct the questionings, his voice tightening in frustration. Moiseyev was insubordinate, refused instruction, rejected counsel, continued to believe and teach an individualized fanatic view for the purpose of undermining the stability and functioning of his unit and division in the Soviet army.

Suddenly Ivan would be dismissed. Somehow, plunged back into a classroom or the middle of a military training session or drill he would have to catch up, take tests, answer questions. If he was unable to perform as required, a complaint would be registered, and Ivan would watch helplessly as an instructor once again entered his name on a shirkers' list.

The winter weeks faded into the spring of 1972 like a blurred, slow-motion nightmare. Exhaustion and cold and uncertainty were wearing him down, Ivan knew. There would be short periods of respite in which days could be passed normally in the army routine before the meetings and interviews and interrogations would begin afresh. Daily Ivan poured out his heart to God.

He had discovered that the door to the storage room for his dormitory was a fire exit and remained unlocked all night. A window on the far wall of the narrow room opened out onto a fire exit running down the side of the building to the street below. With the window open to the breezes from the Black Sea and a chair on which to prop his elbows as he knelt to pray, Ivan passed hours of the mild nights. There was a deep healing in the profound silence of the room. Racks of ghostly uniforms muffled the murmurings of his prayers and tears and whispered hymns from the sleeping soldiers in the dormitory.

Sometimes a homesickness filled him as the fields around the base greened into spring. There were nights that Ivan felt too discouraged to pray. Often of late it seemed his answers to the political leaders and lawyers became confused. He would see by their faces that they had caught him in some statement that pleased them. His mind wandered greatly in the questionings, returning to Moldavia and his parents' small village on the collective farm.

Tonight, the moon from the storage room window sailed a-cross the sky in a stream of clouds. That same moon would have risen over the vineyards of Volontirovka. Ivan was discouraged. Tomorrow he was to appear before breakfast at Malsin's office. "Lord Jesus! Jesus!" The stillness of the room deepened. "Jesus! I don't know how long I can endure!" He had laid his head on his arms on the wooden chair. Sometimes he dozed, waiting for the Lord's hand. A gentle melody hummed in his head, and he let it lull him in the slight warm breeze from the open window. His folded arm muffled his ear and he turned his head slightly to the song. A glint of light caught the lashes of his closed eyes. The music became sweeter.

A familiar shock pulled him to his feet and to the window. The black western sky was bright with an angelic host. Their translucent robes seemed fashioned from glowing lights of different colors and lit their faces with a fierce beauty. They

110

seemed to be moving, but their position in the sky never changed as their song grew and swelled in the night.

> To all the ends of this unhappy earth
> Wherever men be found
> In torrents of pure and mighty faith
> Flows the gospel truth

After a long time their light faded. The sky became less black and slowly grew a pearly grey. It was close to morning. In tears of repentance and happiness Ivan knelt in praise and wonder. A profound stillness hung over the room. Not a bird yet sung. Into his memory an unmistakable Voice spoke. "This is for the comfort of your soul. Tomorrow you will not be questioned. You will soon leave from here."

Malsin was furious that Moiseyev had left the base on a chauffeuring assignment. He had signed an order to stop him. Malsin could not tolerate a blunder in which an order could be lost like a schoolboy's homework! The order would be found and whoever responsible would be punished. His outer office was the scene of an uproar, with clerks turning piles of paper out of drawers and pulling military typists away from their typewriters so wastebaskets could be searched.

"Have you seen the order?"—"Wasn't it late yesterday afternoon that it was sent to the unit sergeant?"—"I haven't got it, as you can see. It has nothing to do with me!" A wire box full of papers was tipped onto the floor, scattering its papers like an aspen tree in a windstorm. More bumping about and exclaiming. A door on the outer office banged. The order was plainly lost.

It was good to be out on the open road, Ivan was thinking,

the vast expanses of fields spread out around them. The truck rolled easily over the asphalt road, its load of bread snug in the back and twice padlocked. A thick hedge of blackthorn bordered this section of the highway, and Ivan glanced at it frequently, enjoying the small birds that darted in and out of the depths of the greenery. The junior officer beside Ivan in the cab was a professional soldier, an agreeable Ukrainian who had managed to buy a melon from a lush kitchen garden as they passed through a tiny village. He was eating it noisily, cutting away the fruit from the rind with the edge of a small pocket knife. From time to time they would pass wooden carts pulled by plodding yoked horses.

Without warning, Ivan heard an inner voice, or thought he did. "Vanya, slow down." He glanced quickly at the speedometer. The needle held steady at sixty kilometers an hour. The Ukranian continued to eat the melon, its juice running off the edge of his chin and falling between his knees.

Impossible that God could be telling him to slow down! They were traveling at a very moderate speed. The hedge was gone now and cool-looking alder thickets followed a long path that led inexplicably into the middle of a field and then disappeared. "Vanya, slow down!"

His eyes lifted to the rear-view mirror. Behind him, as in front, the straight road was empty. Vadim Harmansky tossed his melon rind out the window and wiped his mouth on the back of his sleeve. He closed his knife and placed it in his pocket, raising up slightly in his seat to manage it.

Something bumping along the road caught Ivan's eye. Harmansky exclaimed in astonishment. "Comrade, that's a loaf of our bread!" Another brown object rolled by.

God is stopping us. With a flash of understanding Ivan immediately pulled over and stopped the truck. The officer leaped down from the cab and raced to the back of the vehicle. "Look at this, comrade—the latches are still shut and padlocked!" He looked over his shoulder at the loaves of bread dotting the road as far back as they could see. Rapidly un-

112

locking the truck, the two soldiers stared. Half of their load was gone, strewn over the highway.

Harmansky rubbed the back of his neck in perplexity. "Vanya, tell me. You and I locked these doors together." He shook his head as if clearing out illusions. "All the latches are in place, but the bread is on the road. I have been working on this truck for six years and have never had anything like this happen. It is impossible for these doors to open by themselves. And we closed them together, I remember."

Ivan, too, was perplexed. "And I remember." He stooped to retrieve a loaf of bread. "As we were driving, God told me to slow down, but there seemed to be no reason and I did not obey. He spoke again to my spirit but again I did not obey. Now He has made us stop."

"There are such fables as this in the Scriptures I heard from my babushka as a child." The officer lifted his cap and scratched his head as Ivan eased the truck back on the road and turned it around to go back for the bread. An Ikarus bus full of Black Sea vacationers whizzed past. "My father was a religious Jew. Every Friday night he went to the synagogue in Kiev, and when he was gone, my grandmother would tell me stories by the light of the Sabbath candles. Once she told me of a dream in the Scriptures where a huge loaf of barley bread came tumbling into a camp of the Midian army. It knocked down a whole tent! She said it meant there would be a victory for the Hebrew general." He smiled as he jumped out of the truck to gather up some loaves on the road. As he slammed the cab door and the truck slowly retraced its route, he continued calling, "But what does it mean when God sends a half a load of bread through the back door of a truck?" He laughed sheepishly, but his eyes on Ivan were somber.

"For some reason, God wanted us to slow down. Of that I am sure. When I disregarded Him, He caused the bread to escape to make us stop. I don't know why."

It was a time-consuming job picking up the bread, loaf by loaf, on the quiet road. "Perhaps He did it to punish you!"

Harmansky called across the highway to Ivan. He grinned. "Next time, I'm going to request a different driver.

"You Baptists are a strange lot, Vanya," the sergeant offered as they resumed their route, the dusty bread once again locked safely in the back of the truck. "You don't seem to care what happens to you. Perhaps I believe in God sometimes. I suppose many people do, a little. But what is the purpose of making life miserable by going about broadcasting it to the authorities?"

Ivan answered slowly. "We have freedom of conscience in our country. The Constitution says people may be free to believe or not believe as they like, and to practice religion, or not. There should be no necessity to hide the fact that one believes, comrade."

The officer lit a cigarette impatiently. "You are talking about laws! Don't you realize that the Committee of Public Security* doesn't give a damn about laws?"

Out of habit he lowered his voice. "These are not things I would say to anyone, Vanya, but you are well-liked. Many know you and have heard all you say about God. It is no secret among the common soldiers that some have changed their minds about atheism because of you and what they have seen in your life. They too are now under suspicion." He raised his hand in warning as he saw Ivan about to answer. "For myself I want to be able to say, if I am questioned, that you never spoke to me about religion. Please—do not spoil that."

The officer shifted restlessly, leaning his back against the door of the cab. "But I am telling you. The KGB have been with Malsin and the Polit-Ruk asking questions about you. You are a good lad. I'm not saying I can explain the things that have happened to you. I try not to know about them or think about what I know. But everyone realizes you are a good person. Can you not choose a way to live in which you can stay out of

---

*KGB

114

trouble? What use are you to anyone, shut up for hours and days with the authorities, dragged out of bed, called to interrogations all the time? Eventually you will be destroyed and any good your life could have done will be lost. Surely you have considered that you may be arrested. It's your affair, of course, if you want to throw away your life."

His voice trailed off in horror at the scene approaching them on the road. The Ikarus bus that had passed them as they were gathering bread lay twisted in the roadside ditch. Bodies were strewn in every direction, some caught horribly in an overturned crane into which the bus had apparently collided. Several passenger cars were also crumpled together in what had clearly been a chain reaction. The body of an old man hung grotesquely from a shattered windshield. Police cars and ambulances were beginning to arrive. There was running back and forth through showers of broken glass, slippery with blood. Terrible moaning was coming from all directions.

Ivan and Harmansky sat sickened in the cab of the truck. Harmansky's voice was hollow. "If we had not stopped for the bread, we would have been in this accident. We could have perished. God saved your life." Tears stood in his eyes. His shaking hands were steadied against the instrument panel of the truck.

Ivan spoke with difficulty. "God saved *our* lives." His voice was full of emotion. "It is not only me He loves. It is everybody. It is you, comrade."

Harmansky suddenly bowed his head on his hands and began to weep.

11

*Every cricket
knows its own hearth.*

Malsin spit out the piece of fingernail he had just torn with his teeth and sucked the raw edge of cuticle. His hands were sore, he was sick from excessive smoking and before him on his desk was once again the opened file of Ivan Moiseyev. Yet another report would have to be made, this time on the disturbance caused by Moiseyev and Comrade Officer Harmansky on their return to the base in the bread truck. Already there were far too many incidents, recorded, unexplained, uncorrected.

Clearly there was to be no end to the incidents. What was he to write? "Normal routine on the base was disrupted last week by reports by Ivan Moiseyev and Vadim Harmansky that God had propelled army bread from their locked vehicle to the road in order to detain them and thus prevent their involvement in a serious accident." Malsin himself had investigated the crowd of soldiers forming around the bread delivery truck. Harmansky had been weeping as he told the story. Obviously he had suffered a nervous collapse. A new thought disturbed Malsin. Perhaps he should have had Harmansky arrested for negligence. It was quite obviously a case of irresponsibility that he had not locked the back of the truck. He shrugged. Now that he was with psychiatrists, better to leave it at that.

But why did it have to happen with Moiseyev? Always Moiseyev.

The Office of Special Affairs had verified the bus accident and this added to the excitement on the base. Moiseyev was a genius at being able to exploit a situation in order to claim yet another miracle for his God.

In spite of every reeducation procedure, Moiseyev continued to propagate his views. Malsin had been gratified to discover that at least Moiseyev had attended an unregistered congregation in Moldavia. A criminal case could probably be made of that but it was now far in the past. It was Moiseyev's deliberate program of disobedience that ate at Malsin day and night. Repeatedly he had been ordered to be silent about his religious beliefs. The military and polit-officers had worked with him in every legal way. And in other ways as well.

A May breeze from the open window scattered cigarette ashes over the papers on the desk. Malsin continued to stare at the pile of Moiseyev reports, not bothering to brush off the ashes.

The situation was becoming embarrassingly difficult to manage. The report from the military hospital in Simferopol with its official seal was under his hand. Two hundred men in the harvest convoy last autumn claimed to believe some sort of supernatural healing of Moiseyev's injuries. No doubt they were influenced by stories filtering down from the surgeon-general's office. The memory of the surgeon's shaken voice on the telephone still rankled Malsin. "For the first time in my life I see that there really is a God!" What kind of doctors did they have in Simferopol? Not people of science. Malsin wouldn't take an animal there! He lit another cigarette. It had been good fortune that the men in that convoy had been from many units in differing cities. What if the convoy had been entirely from Kerch? Two hundred men returning to the base with wild-eyed stories of miracles!

All happenings had natural causes. In the matter of Moiseyev standing in the snow: perhaps he had some innate ability to withstand cold. In the war it had been known that some men had been able to achieve superhuman feats. Instead of bravery, heroism sometimes turned out to be a matter of a man's not hearing an order or being too thick-headed to understand a strategy. Sometimes it was a genetic accident that rendered a man a momentary advantage over his fellows, like color blindness or short stature in the foxholes. Perhaps genetics could explain Moiseyev. Certainly he had withstood incredible cold and pressure in the reeducation sessions in the prison at Sverdlovsk—that is, if the reports sent to him from Sverdlovsk could be believed. Malsin's cigarette burned to its end. He stubbed it out impatiently in the overflowing tray.

There was no question that Moiseyev must be brought to a formal trial. For eighteen incredible months he had openly defied the Red army and withstood the most dedicated political efforts at reeducation. His insistence that he had not broken any Soviet laws but was suffering as a believer was a direct slander against the Soviet state and social order. That too was reason enough for arrest. The Constitution of the USSR guaranteed the freedom of conscience of all Soviet citizens. Religious persecution did not take place in the USSR.

Malsin was tired. He had been sleeping poorly. It was inconvenient, but a case would have to be made against Moiseyev, his illegal activities, his open preaching of religion, his defiance of Soviety reality. Dolotov had made it clear that a person with such views could never be released from the Red army. He had reminded Malsin that one of the functions of the military was to cleanse society of impulse movements that act against the interests of the working class. A tribunal would be arranged. With only six months left of Moiseyev's service, he had to be tried and sentenced and sent away long before the question of his discharge came up. Malsin rang the small bell on his desk. After several moments the door of the office opened slowly and the private on duty looked in.

Malsin cleared his throat impatiently. He disliked the fact that the private was a soldier from Moiseyev's unit. "Get me Ivan Moiseyev. I want him in my office immediately."

The door closed quickly, then reopened. The private looked uncertain. "I'm sorry, sir. Moiseyev left yesterday for Moldavia for his second-year leave. He won't be back for eight days, until the twelfth, sir."

"Damn it!" Malsin screamed his fury and fatigue. "How is it possible that special cases like Moiseyev are processed along with everyone else? How is it possible that I was not consulted? I never intended him to go home on leave!" Malsin was staring so furiously at the private, advancing on him with every question, that the soldier paled in apprehension. "I don't know, sir. I'm sorry there was some mistake."

"Get out of here!" Malsin's voice was strangled with rage. It was not possible to do a job surrounded by incompetence. His wife was at work. He would go home. Stuffing his papers into his briefcase from a table beside his desk, he walked purposefully out of the room, the determination that he would soon bring the Moiseyev disturbance to a conclusion filling him with new energy.

All the windows of the small log house were wide open to the sweetness of the spring Sunday morning. Air was needed, for the believers crowded inside. The young people leaned against the window sills outside, their voices carrying the singing across the lush fields and pleasant meadows. Not a believer was missing this morning because brother Ivan was home from the army on leave. Young Svetlana Petrovna strained at the window to get a glimpse of Ivan as he sat in a place of honor at the front of the room with the pastors. He was dressed in the same clothes he had always worn to the meetings, but he looked years older. Svetlana wondered if she had changed so much. They were singing the Moldavian hymns everyone loved, one after another. It was a way of celebrating Ivan's return and encouraging him. Svetlana joined in with all her heart. She had heard Ivan had been having a difficult time.

Several of the pastors would speak, but before the meeting was over Svetlana knew that Ivan would be asked to preach. She leaned her chin on the sill and gazed at all the Moiseyevs sitting together near the pastors. Every one of their faces shone with excitement and joy. Even some unbelieving neighbors became curious and were pressing against the young people at the windows, trying to see inside. A woman Svetlana knew to be a foreman at the silk factory pulled her back from the window. "What's special today?" she demanded. "What's going on in there?"

Some other village people pushed past the young people and jostled at the windows to watch. Nina Kopnik, a cousin of Svetlana's, sighed in exasperation. All the young people had given up their positions by the window. "But unbelievers will hear the gospel," Svetlana whispered. "Be glad."

After the singing, Ivan was invited by the pastors to speak first. He began to read Old Testament verses from a borrowed Bible.

" 'Then the Lord opened the eyes of Balaam and he saw the angel of the Lord standing in the way with his sword drawn in his hand; and he bowed all the way to the ground.' " Ivan raised his eyes from the small book with a radiant smile. "Even so today God can reveal His angels to His followers and demonstrate His power." The silk factory foreman by the window shifted her weight, her eyes upon Ivan in fascination. Svetlana caught a glimpse of his expression of loving earnestness. "I should also like to quote Mark 14:35, which says, 'And He went a little beyond them, and fell to the ground and began praying that, if it were possible, the hour might pass Him by.' So, dear brothers and sisters, such hours of trouble that come to us do represent times of great difficulty, and many of us have these experiences. In such an hour the Lord resorted to prayer. He was aware of all that awaited Him, but *we* have no such awareness. Instead of a sermon, I should like to invite you to pray. As the Lord Jesus prayed, so let us engage in prayer."

Something in his voice made Svetlana's eyes smart with tears. The foreman and some others moved away with a shrug. It was nothing exceptional after all. The Baptists were always praying. Svetlana moved forward with the other young people, back to their places at the windows. So Ivan was not going to preach. Instead he had asked that they pray.

It was after the long service that the adults made way for the young to find places around Ivan, filling the already cramped living room to overflowing. There was shyness in the welcome of the young people. No one wanted to ask embarrassing questions, yet everyone wanted to know the details of his difficulties. Someone softly closed the open windows and the front door. An old grandmother sitting next to Ivan holding his arm suddenly jogged him. "Vanya, Vanya," her old voice cracked with loving emotion. "Tell us how it has been."

It was an afternoon Svetlana would never forget. What wonderful things the Lord had done! The miracle of the healing! Of the bread! Of the sergeant's leave! Often hymns of praise began in response to Ivan's stories. Sometimes a brother or sister would pray for Ivan's officers, for the new brothers in the army Ivan told about, for the other soldiers who had heard the gospel. At times their voices would fall silent, and Ivan, his face lit with the happiness of being home, would speak again of the wonderful works of God.

Dusk was falling as the Moiseyevs made their way along the rolling dirt road from the prayer house in Slabodzeya to their own village of Volontirovka. The younger boys were drowsy, stumbling beside their mother, oblivious to the beauty of the gentle light gilding the curve of the hills and the young green of the treetops. His sister and two of the older boys were softly singing hymns, every once in a while glancing over their shoulders with a smile for Ivan as they sang. Each tree and path and fence that they passed was achingly familiar to Ivan. As they walked he could see in the distance the house of his married brother near the small thicket where he had hunted mushrooms in the summers.

His father, keeping pace with him, walked silently, unwilling to disturb the memories that were almost visible on his son's face. An oriole making its three-note call pierced the air with sweetness. "It's so beautiful." Ivan's voice was low, as if he feared to break the hush of the twilight. Vasiliy Trofimovich smiled indulgently. Far off in the fields he could see the heavy equipment of the collective farm waiting to begin the morning's cultivation. Abruptly Ivan stopped walking and grasped his father's arms, his eyes wet. "It's hard, Papa. I want you to know. I'll never see Moldavia again."

Such things as tape recorders and microphones were as foreign to the tiny Moiseyev cottage as they would have been in the court at Saint Petersburg in the days of the czars. But Brother Zheluak from Slabodzeya had appeared with his machine on Ivan's last evening home, enthused about a plan. For years Zheluak had taped the Christian radio broadcasts he received on his shortwave radio, replaying them for his family and for the believers after the services. It would be a simple matter to record Ivan telling of his experiences in the army. Why should the few believers in the Suvorovskiy region be the only ones to hear the wonderful things the Lord had done for Ivan in the army? A tape could be made and carried by the pastors all over Moldavia and played in congregation after congregation. What glory to God and what encouragement to the brethren!

For some reason, when Ivan began the taping, Joanna Constantinova began to weep. The months had been difficult for her as she had read and reread between the lines of Ivan's letters home. Vasiliy had hoped that seeing Ivan would have quieted her fears, but since Ivan's return his wife had hardly slept, staring at her son with a face so full of concern that even Ivan had laughed. "Momma, I think you will battle the whole Red army for me," he had teased, adding, "These things are in the hands of God. You must pray, yes, but we may not choose for ourselves what is to be. What God wills, shall be. Our concern is only to be worthy of Him." Joanna had tried to smile when she met Ivan's glance, but there was a detachment about him that filled her nights with fear and her days with dread. Nothing must happen to him. He was her son.

12

In the land of the naked, people are ashamed of clothes.

Malsin paced his small apartment restlessly, walking from window to window, glancing down at the busy Kerch street watching for the quick figure of his wife making her way through the crowds. His ten-year-old son was already bent over his homework spread out on the table in the living room. He worked quietly, occasionally raising his head to observe his father's impatience.

"Momma will be home soon." He had his mother's way of soothing. "I expect she stopped for some vegetables at the market."

Malsin nodded, throwing himself into a chair.

It was going better with the Moiseyev affair. He was pleased. But Galina should be here. He wanted to tell her what a good thing it had been after all that Moiseyev had gone home on leave. The interval had given him time to think, to plan a strategem, to confer with the district Polit-Ruk, to see the issues with clarity. The boy looked up again from his books, his pale blue eyes full of light. "Momma's home!"

Galina Ivanova kicked the apartment door shut with her foot, swinging the string bag full of beetroot onto the kitchen table and dumping an armful of small parcels alongside. She eyed her husband apprehensively, recovered herself, and smiled warmly at the boy in the next room.

"Would you like some tea?" Automatically she moved to the sink with the kettle, her bare arms already slightly tanned from the hot spring sun.

Malsin reached in his pocket for a cigarette. "Yes, tea would be welcome." He inhaled deeply. "You'll be happy to know I'm feeling very pleased about the Moiseyev business."

Galina placed the kettle on the gas flame with elaborate

carefulness. In an effort to be calm, she sat down in the chair opposite her husband. The beetroot and parcels on the table made a wall between them. "We had agreed not to discuss the matter."

"But the difficulty lay in the fact that I was uncertain as to how to proceed. It is no ordinary case. His uncanny ability to resist discipline, to create bizarre incidents, to publicize his fanaticism have been most unusual. It came to me that what was essential was to work out to the last detail all questions concerning the progression of his case. It was a very good thing, after all, that he was sent home on leave. His absence gave me a needed respite. I have planned a strategem with the utmost of precision."

"A strategem." Galina moved toward the steaming kettle, mechanically pouring the boiling water into the small samovar that had been a wedding present years ago. How much they both had changed.

Malsin pushed the packages aside to put down the cup of tea his wife handed to him. "Of course this has been on your mind, Galina, making you nervous. It has been hanging over our head for months. How do you think I know you haven't slept well? I haven't slept. It is a miracle that I haven't had to give an explanation to the *Spetz-Otdel** before this for the irregularities up to now. There seems to be no end of the tricks this Rasputin with the innocent face can pull out of his bag."

His wife's cup remained invisible behind the groceries. "A miracle," she repeated. Malsin became irritated at the disagreeable way she was staring at him, repeating his words.

"I understood that the Communist Party does not believe in miracles. You have a strange vocabulary."

"I am trying to remember that you too have been under a strain because of this. I came home to tell you that the difficulties with Moiseyev will soon be resolved. I have taken

---

Spetzialnij-Otdel ("Special Department," or KGB).

decisive action. This morning he returned to Kerch. Already he has been arrested. I assumed that it might put your mind at ease to know that together with the security agents a procedure has been established, and he has been formally arrested."

"I don't want to know the procedure. I don't want to know about Moiseyev. I've told you many times not to talk about him to me."

It was difficult not to despise the incredible weakness in women. Even today there were very few women who had achieved the socialist ideal of objectivity necessary for full liberation. Malsin had once hoped Galina was such a woman.

"The problem has been that Moiseyev is quite willing to go openly to prison. He is so lost in the labyrinth of his imagination that it is of no concern to him where he is. One place will do as well as another for his anti-Soviet activities, his Baptist preaching, his 'miracles' to flourish. What a victory! For the Red army to provide such a preacher for the prison camps!" Malsin inhaled deeply. "Every man has his breaking point. Moiseyev has his. That is the point we have determined to reach."

Fury choked Galina Ivanova's voice to a whisper. "I have told you not to tell me these things. I have told you I will not stand them." In a flash she was in front of the sink with her tea. Deliberately she raised the cup and smashed it against the side. The saucer followed with redoubled violence.

In a reflex of rage Malsin struck his wife in a swing of his hand that spun her against the kitchen wall. With the return of his arm he grabbed his briefcase and was in the hall of the apartment, staring at her reddening face and defiant eyes. Deliberately he reached into the room for the side of the door, slamming it at her violently. In a freezing calm, he walked slowly into the gentle sunshine. Galina be damned.

In spite of the clement time of the year, the cell was cold. High in the wall, near the ceiling the small window was outlined in a brilliant blue. Outside, the sky stretched above the prison, over the city of Simferopol, and further, a vast canopy for fields and hills bursting with early summer for dazzling rivers and at last the fragrant vineyards of Moldavia.

Ivan had been staring for hours at the window. He finally pulled his eyes away from the blue and tried to pray. A feeling of weightlessness, disembodiment plagued him. It was as if real life had stopped and he was suspended in the cell, unable to feel that the events taking place around him were genuine. Was it a melodrama of his imagination that he might die? Had Malsin actually meant that he was neither to be sentenced to prison or discharged from the army if he refused to change his convictions? Surely he had misunderstood. The Russian language was difficult. Possibly sometimes he did not understand.

All along it had not been death he had feared, but the possibility of denying Christ, denying the angelic visions, the healing of his body, the love of God that had many times literally filled his body with life-giving heat. He was unsure what might be done to a man behind the closed doors of special cells to make him recant, blaspheme, embrace all that he abhorred. It was his own weakness that he feared.

But something like the lingering of a shadow seemed to pervade his cell. It was impossible to be rid of the one tormenting thought that was recurring in a thousand different forms: In the end, his dying would accomplish nothing. In renewed anguish Ivan paced his cell. If it came to dying, if he withstood, if it were possible by God's power he were able to withstand, then he would be gone. No more than that. A torment of loss wrenched his mind. Once his future had stretched before him with the promise of goodness and mercy all the days of his life. Images of his family, his home, his friends, his country pushed upon him. He began to think of the bride he would never have. Small faces of children floated in the air of his cell.

"I am going mad!" It was said that religion caused madness. Desperately Ivan fixed his mind upon Scripture. "Save me, O God. For the waters have come up to my soul. I have sunk in deep mire and there is no foothold; I have come into deep waters, and a flood overflows me. I am weary with my crying; my throat is parched; my eyes fail while I wait for my God. Those who hate me are more than the hairs of my head; those who would destroy me are powerful.

"O God, it is Thou who dost know my folly, and my wrongs are not hidden from Thee. May those who wait for Thee not be ashamed through me, O Lord God of hosts. May those who seek Thee not be dishonored through me, O Lord God of Israel."

The face of Prokhorov, the Armenian sergeant, flashed into his mind. He saw again the wonderful smile with which he had greeted Ivan after his return from the harvest fields. Over and over he had embraced Ivan, kissing him on both cheeks, embracing him again, calling him "my brother." He had joyously kept his promise to believe. The memory of Prokhorov eased Ivan's pain. He sat quietly on the metal cot in his cell. Many had believed. His flesh shrunk back from the ordeal ahead, but would not God prove faithful? "Steadfast, steadfast!" Ivan said aloud. "You go forward on Christ's orders."

The military prosecutor in Simferopol had assembled the same bewildering and familiar charges that Ivan had heard so many times before from officers of the Kerch Polit-Ruk. Under article 142 he was charged with violating the codex in being a member of an unregistered Baptist congregation in Moldavia. In Kerch itself he had attended unregistered meetings in hours the army had provided for his rest and relaxation. According to article 190, paragraph 1, of the criminal code he was further charged with the distribution of literature containing deliberately false statements slandering the Soviet state. A letter to his parents was produced which included the reference that he was suffering for Christ. "Freedom of conscience is guaranteed to every citizen of the USSR. You have deliberately besmirched the Soviet Union and the Red army." The tribunal officer had picked up a small paper and began to read a few lines. "The Decree of Lenin, Point Five: 'Free celebration of religious rites is guaranteed insofar as they do not disturb public order and do not infringe the rights of citizens of the Soviet republic.' " He gave Ivan a measured look before continuing. "Repeatedly, Comrade Moiseyev, you have infringed upon the rights of your fellow soldiers in your unit and company and in other units with which you have had contact. Your continuous observance of prayer and preaching are intolerable to others around you. You have been repeatedly ordered to desist from this harassment of others, but have refused. Your religious observations on state property have violated the regulations on the separation of church and state. You are condemned, not by this tribunal, but by your own actions. Still, an opportunity is being given to you today to accept the judgment of this court, to confess your anti-Soviet activity and publicly change your views. You will be given three days to think it over."

From Simferopol he had been returned to Kerch for the three-day waiting period, then taken to the military prison there. Again the interrogations began, with Major Gidenko and Captain Yarmak reading the lists of accusations, shouting that it would be at Kerch that he would spend his seven years in prison. Ivan shifted uneasily in the prisoner's dock. Gidenko was giving him another three-day ultimatum. Why was it that the courts were unwilling to sentence him? He had told everyone repeatedly that he was ready to accept prison.

Malsin yawned. It had been a long session with Gidenko and he had stayed throughout. He had not been to his apartment since the argument with Galina. He entertained the idea of going home, then rejected it. The Moiseyev matter required his full attention. The strategy that had been planned needed to be carried out with absolute precision and without the incredible blundering that had plagued this case from the beginning. By staying on the job he had seen the matter through this far. He wasn't going to rest now.

131

With a feeling of satisfaction Malsin checked off the progress this far. Moiseyev had already seen Commissar Dolotov in Simferopol and been charged. Since he had not pleaded guilty, he was returned to the Polit-Ruk at Kerch where he had a hearing and was examined by his own polit-officers. Again, a deadline was given to him. If he failed to comply (and Malsin was certain he would), he would be sent for examination to the district Polit-Ruk in Odessa before being returned to Simferopol for what Malsin called "the final outcome." It was of little importance that the interrogations and threats had not proved successful this far. Malsin shrugged. It was of little importance to him at what stage Moiseyev broke. Break he would. In a short time he would be entering the special session phase at Simferopol.

It was becoming difficult for Ivan to remember what day it was. There had been so much shunting back and forth between prisons and hearings and the base at Kerch that he was losing track of time. He stood unsteadily once again in the Simferopol prisoner's dock, his face pale. Already the tan with which he had returned from Moldavia had receded into a prisoner's pallor. He was hungry. He had been abused by the guards. He had had little sleep in the past two weeks. The officers gazed impassively at him, waiting his testimony. His voice was hoarse from weariness, but he tried to speak distinctly in the still unfamiliar Russian.

"I plead not guilty to the charges against me and I ask again to speak to the tribunal."

Commissar Dolotov's mournful face nodded in assent.

"When I was drafted into the army, I took the oath of loyalty and I have tried never to break my promise to give full allegiance and obedience to the military of the USSR. There have been orders I have received that it was impossible for me to obey, orders I believe that are improper and violate the Constitution's guarantee of freedom of conscience. I did not obey these orders, not because I am disloyal to the Red army,

132

but because they were improper, and most of all because I have one higher allegiance, and that is to Jesus Christ. He has given me certain orders, and these I cannot disobey."

Dolotov spoke with quiet interest. "You have received particularized orders from Jesus Christ?"

"No more than any Christian in that we are told to tell what great things the Lord has done for us, to be witnesses to His glory where we are. Comrade commissar, I have never harassed others with the preaching of the gospel. Where there has been interest, I have spoken of the love of God and His care of me and all those who love Him. I don't consider it a crime to give bread to the hungry. Many of the things that have happened to me and to others are miracles. In our day many say there is no God, yet He is doing miracles because he loves all men and wants all men to be saved. The only religious observances in which I have engaged on the base is prayer, and what law forbids Soviet citizens to pray? You tell me not to talk about my faith, but the love of God cannot be hidden. It is written, 'If I say, "I will not remember Him or speak any more in His name," then in my heart it becomes like a burning fire shut up in my bones; and I am weary of holding it in.' I do not ask this tribunal for mercy, because mercy comes from God. I am ready to accept prison with joy. I have been told my sentence is to be seven years. Then let me receive it. Another period for me to reconsider is useless. I cannot deny God who has given me so much happiness. I can only praise Him."

Without a word, Dolotov nodded brusquely to the guard. Malsin controlled the irritation that scalded his stomach. He must be patient. All was going according to plan, even though Moiseyev's composure could be infuriating. Signaling to the security agents of the Spetz-Otdel, who had been observing from a small table at the back of the room, Malsin carried a chair to their table and sat down. His smile was thin, but he made an effort at sociability. "It is simply a matter of time, comrades. At this moment he is on his way to the prison security units for as long as it takes."

133

13

*Death does not take
the old, but the ripe.*

With growing certainty, Ivan was becoming aware of what was ahead. The tribunals had repeatedly threatened him with imprisonment if he did not change his views, only to extend his deadline when he refused. As clearly as possible Ivan had said, "Jesus Christ has given me the order to proclaim His word in whatever city I am in, in my military unit, and to officers and soldiers. I must follow His order." Still his sentence was withheld.

At first Ivan had thought the authorities were considering the reactions of the men in his unit if he were sent to prison. Many soldiers had believed. And many more declared that God exists and that they had seen miracles. Even Sergei had become a center of attention in his own unit. Soldiers sought him out to ask questions, to pray with him, to read his Scripture portions. Ivan sighed. A longing to see Sergei haunted him. Repeatedly he had asked that Sergei be permitted to visit him, but his guards and cells were changed so frequently that he was unsure that the request had been delivered to the officials. Sergei and many of the soldiers would be praying for him, Ivan knew. But the authorities would not be afraid of their reactions. Multiple arrests were common after a sentence had been passed.

Repeatedly the Lord had spoken to him. "Jesus Christ is going into battle." Yes, he knew that. Had not the days since his return from leave been a battle? Water lay in pools on the floor of his new cell. The air was foul. For breakfast he had had no bread. Was this not a struggle? Was he not fighting down his fears, his longings for a natural life, his dread of the unknown? Was he not enduring the strain of repeated threats, hearings, interrogations, deadlines, movings from prison to prison, from cell to cell? Was he not witnessing to the guards, to the interrogators? But something assured him the battle was not to be prison.

This cell was wet, and had no bed. It reminded him painfully of the cell in Sverdlovsk where he had hunched over a year ago. He shuddered, remembering the nightmare progression of cells: the cubicle with icy water pouring from the ceiling, and after that, the refrigerated cell, and then the agony of the pressure suit. "Jesus Christ is going into battle." As the words turned over and over in his mind an overwhelming sense of Presence jarred him alert. Joy spread gently through him, warming, burning, bringing him to his knees in the water. "For Me you are to do battle. But be of good cheer. I am with you. I have overcome the world." "Jesus Christ is going into battle." He had overcome the world. Ivan, too, *would* overcome. His questions fled. There would be no prison sentence and no discharge. Tears soaked Ivan's face. He bowed as low as he could in the cramped space, and wept and worshiped.

A guard making his rounds glanced into the cell with interest. This was something he could report to the tribunal. With the stub of a pencil he wrote in his book, "Moiseyev lying in the water, weeping." The guard hoped this was a good sign. Perhaps the young soldier would break before long.

It was bad business drawing it out. They called it a fancy name, but it was torture, all the same.

For ten days Ivan endured agony, at the end deliriously praying for death and the release the Lord had promised him. Finally the tribunal refused to continue. Malsin had been beside himself with fury at their report. "It is our judgment that persuasive efforts are futile. This prisoner can be quickly sentenced and sent away. Continuance of security efforts will produce unpredictable results." In other words, if the procedures were to continue, let the "results" be the responsibility of the KGB and not the Simferopol tribunal. But it was not according to plan! Malsin had an intense headache. He had made his plans with precision. It had not been his intention to return to the base with Moiseyev unbroken.

The coffee shop in the prison was a filthy place, the few tables smeared and sticky with a bitter smell of rotting cloth about them. Malsin longed for vodka as he stirred his thick coffee with a tin spoon. The KGB were planning to continue the program by working Moiseyev over in their branch headquarters in Kerch. Perhaps turning it over to them was for the best after all. A military tribunal had to have legal scruples which were unnecessary in the security force. The KGB had sanction to act administratively, to overrule courts of law and close legal loopholes when necessary for the security of the working people. Malsin pulled himself heavily to his feet. His headache was killing him.

It was a few days before Moiseyev was recovered enough to return to Kerch, where he was placed in special quarters. Malsin was anxious for everything to appear as normal as possible. No incidents must occur with the enlisted men. Malsin adapted his plan with elaborate care, concentrating in spite of the headache that would not go away.

It was in the middle of the night when he remembered when the headache had begun. The interrogator in Simferopol had placed Ivan's foot in a freezer unit. It had been a superfluous idea. Malsin disapproved of such warning procedures. Moiseyev should have been placed immediately in the cell freezer unit itself. The shock alone would have been as effective as the below-zero temperatures, especially for an already weakened constitution. But the foot incident had served to indicate that his speculations about Moiseyev's unusual cold endurance had been correct. Where any normal man would be screaming with pain, Moiseyev continued his maddening praying and claimed to feel only some pain. It was obvious his foot was frozen. Malsin reached for the vodka on his bedside table and corrected himself. It was obvious that any normal person's foot would be frozen. The interrogator insisted it was frozen, that the equipment was in perfect order. In spite of his deteriorated condition, Moiseyev had turned the incident into another one of his miracles. God, of course, had healed his foot in answer to prayer. It was the look of fear on the interrogator's face that had given Malsin this infernal headache. He drank quickly for the maximum effect of the alcohol. It didn't matter.

Well, he had given Moiseyev a last deadline. And tomorrow it was up. He poured another drink in the dark. Soon, he would go home to Galina and young Sasha. All the unpleasantness would be over. Galina would be happy. He fell into a restless sleep, dimly aware of the dull, throbbing pain that drummed in the back of his consciousness.

All the morning of July 16, he was detained by a delegation of party officials from Yugoslavia. He had expected them to be handled by any one of the other senior officers, but the instructions from Odessa had specified that Lt. Col. V.I. Malsin was to extend the courtesies of Kerch and conduct the delegation on a tour of the base. It was madness to be describing military training methods, political science curriculums, and programs of leaves while the morning hours wore away with Moiseyev at liberty.

Today was the last deadline. Today pressure would be applied until Moiseyev broke. Malsin had great difficulty keeping his mind on the Yugoslavs. He could hardly restrain the rush of triumph that filled him when he thought of Moiseyev standing in the packed auditorium of the base's Palace of Culture, humbly repudiating his religious views, confessing his slanders against the Soviet state. Let the soldiers who had sunk into belief see their leader then! Perhaps Moiseyev should appeal for clemency and the opportunity to correct the views of the men he had led into error. That would make an impressive report for Dolotov.

Around noon he was able to excuse himself from the farewell amenities with the Yugoslav delegates because of "pressing business." The officers of the KGB had been waiting most of the morning in Malsin's office. He was astonished at their calmness. Now that there was the pressure of time, he was gratified that he had worked out a precise plan. Every detail had been thought of. The secrecy that had been possible in Simferopol would be maintained in Kerch. There would be no rumors or speculations among the soldiers of Moiseyev's unit.

Moiseyev would drive himself to the KGB headquarters in the city as if he were on an ordinary assignment. Malsin and the civilian security officers would leave the base in a Pobeda. A sense of exultation stirred Malsin. It was unfortunate, of course, that severe measures had to be taken. But keeping the end in view—the cleansing of men's minds, the building of pure socialism—there were times when these procedures were required. And the KGB were experts. With a glance at his watch, Malsin picked up the telephone to order the cars. In a matter of minutes they would have Moiseyev in the special soundproof office of the security police. Today he would break!

Somehow it had never seriously occurred to Malsin that Moiseyev would prefer to die. The eventuality had not been in his plans. His death was of no concern to the KGB, of course. They had anticipated it as a probability. But for Malsin, the brutal end of the work swept away his dream of victory.

He had been sweating heavily during the frenzied afternoon. Now he was shaking with cold in spite of the July heat, his mouth dry with fear. His head was exploding. He stared unbelieving at Moiseyev's motionless body on the floor of the soundproof room. There would be explanations to provide, reports to make out, the boy's parents to notify, and the soldiers in his unit to satisfy. The believer, Sergei, could be detained. But how could Moiseyev's death be explained to the soldiers?

The KGB men were silently cleaning up the room. Malsin stood erect, controlling his trembling with folded arms across his chest. He wanted to sit down, to lie down. If only there were time to go over what had gone wrong, to listen again to what Moiseyev had said before his moans and prayers were silenced. "Christ . . . loves all sinners." Was that what he had said?

Small trickles of blood continued to ooze from the puncture wounds around his heart. The KGB were confident that he was not yet dead and that his death could be made to appear an accident. They were treating Malsin like some kind of fool, moving him out of the way, deftly wrapping Moiseyev in a blanket. Surely there was a doctor for a headache like this. Malsin sat down, holding his head. Let them drown Moiseyev if they liked. The Black Sea was close enough. Malsin felt there was something he had to remember. If only the pounding would stop. It was something Moiseyev had said.

14

*The straight
can't become straighter.*

From the moment she had held the terrible telegram in her hand Joanna Constantinova determined not to cry. It was as if a cannonball had torn through her, leaving so little of herself behind that giving in to tears would forever waste what ebbing strength she had. White-faced, she sent a child speeding to the fields for her husband. Another son, as frightened as his brother, ran to the collective director to tell that his mother would not be at work. Joanna tried to think. There were things to be done, arrangements to be made if they were to claim Ivan's body.

Her eyes had been dry during the long hot journey to Kerch. The fields on both sides of the creaking train lay basking in the blinding yellow glare of the torrid sun. She wondered that Semyon could stare so long at the shimmering landscape.

It was right that Semyon, the oldest, should come with them to help with the arrangements, but Joanna wished he had stayed at home. It was oppressive not to be able to speak freely to her husband when her heart was bursting with pain. Semyon believed too heartily in the telegram, imagining aspects of the drowning, sometimes repeating anguished questions as he gazed at the moving countryside. "How could he have drowned with comrades present? Why could he not have been revived? Why did such a senseless accident have to happen?"

At such moments Joanna glared at her husband in hopeless anger. What opportunity did a village boy from Volontirovka have to learn to swim? The whole family knew Ivan couldn't swim. If there had never been any letters, if he had never come home on leave with his stories of what was really happening, every one of them still would have heard the drowning accident strike a false note.

Joanna was surprised at the size of Kerch, its seaport streets crowded with sailors as well as soldiers, the smell of fish and the screams of gulls mixing with the sounds of traffic and filling the city air. Her thin face was flushed from the hotness of her black dress and black kerchief in the July heat. Her husband and son moved more easily through the crowded streets, directed by an ice cream seller to the bus stop that would take them to the military base.

She had not expected to meet Colonel Malsin himself. She clung tightly to her husband's arm, her mind a torment as he spoke. Surely the Moiseyevs would have some tea. There were some official procedures to take care of, but their son Semyon could prove helpful in the situation. The army wished to burden the grieving parents as little as possible. It had been a terrible shock.

It seemed to have been a terrible shock to the colonel also. Joanna watched his trembling hands and drawn face with astonishment. He was shaking Semyon's hand, making what appeared to be an enormous effort at civility. Semyon was a member of the Komsomol in his Suvorovskiy region of Moldavia. Excellent. A fine son. He could assist in the military arrangements and permit his parents rest after their long journey. Malsin walked a few steps with Semyon toward his office. Coming back, he stood hesitantly before the parents. A strange moment passed before he nodded toward a cluster of chairs in his outer office. Apprehensively, Joanna sat down beside her husband. Malsin's voice was husky with smoke and fatigue.

Joanna had difficulty hearing him and understanding his Russian. A burning cigarette smoldered in his hand. "Comrades Vasiliy and Joanna Moiseyev, there's something for you to know." He lowered his voice even further and spoke haltingly. "I was present when your son died. He fought with death. He died hard, but he died a Christian." The word hung in the stuffy outer office. Joanna gazed in stupifaction at the colonel. Had she understood? What an incredibly strange thing for an officer in the Red army to say. Her husband's steady voice broke the silence. "Thank you for telling us. We had no question in our minds about that. The Lord is faithful unto death."

Malsin turned and strode uneasily into his office. What was the matter with him? Why did he feel impelled to talk about Moiseyev? He had drowned. That was the important thing to remember. He must concentrate on that fact. He would discuss everything with Galina when he went home. Telling her would get it out of his system. He closed his office door and gazed at Semyon. As a member of the Young Communist League there could be no question as to where his loyalties lay. He must be made to fully understand his responsibilities. Malsin took a deep breath and lit another cigarette.

A hot night breeze was blowing in the slightly open window of the train as they had traveled back to Volontirovka. Joanna had not been surprised that Semyon had said not a word to them about his long interview with Malsin. The lights inside the car made mirrors of the train windows and Joanna stared at the reflection of her son in the window. The small crescent of the summer moon in the black sky outside over his head appeared like a sickle. The car was crowded with tired holidayers, some nodding in sleep, others sharing sausage slices or bits of cheese from bundles they carried with them. But Semyon sat erect, staring at the screen of night that had dropped over the window. His hair fell over his face like stone. Not a part of him moved.

Once during the night he had turned from the window with a long look at his parents. His eyes rested on his father, bent forward in his seat in prayer. Without speaking, he glanced at his mother and turned silently back to his window. Something in the brief tableau was so like the shutting of a door that Joanna turned her head impulsively to the door of the passenger car. Had it suddenly closed? It was her imagination.

The closing had been in Semyon. At that moment, she finally began to weep. In some way she didn't understand, Semyon too was gone.

They would carry his body through the village in an open coffin as was the custom. Joanna Constantinova's weeping continued from the other side of the crowded room as the men prepared Ivan for the funeral. The unfamiliar smell of flash bulbs hung in the hot air as the pastors worked in silence, lifting and straining against the unyielding weight of the corpse as they dressed it in village clothes. What was the use of taking a picture of what the army had done to him? Joanna tried to sip from the glass of water that the sister beside her on the couch urged upon her, but then pushed it away. Someone wiped her face.

Joanna closed her aching eyes. In the room, the brothers were gathering up Ivan's uniform and motioning the sisters to bring the flowers for the inside of the coffin. Involuntarily her eyes opened again at the sound of shuffling. A paper was brought forward. Faintly Joanna remembered that Vasiliy had been preparing a statement for people to sign. He was determined to have it shown and witnessed that his son's corpse did not correspond with the death certificate of "mechanical asphyxiation" that Officer Platonov had delivered. The burns, the stab wounds, the marks of beatings would be verified before burial. But who would dare to believe it, even if it were signed by all Moldavia? Vasiliy was bending over, tenderly speaking her name. Under his name, she added her own. Dully she watched Vasiliy moving about with the document. There was so much one didn't need to explain. Wisely, he was giving the pen not only to the believers present, but also to the other neighbors and villagers in the room.

Seemingly without direction the believers began to sing. Joanna rose awkwardly, helped by the sisters who sat with her on the small couch. The hymn, "I Am a Pilgrim," streamed out the open windows to the streets and fragrant summer fields beyond. Many from the village were already inside the tiny house. More stood outside, listening at the open shutters and against the side of the cottage. There would be one or two gospel messages, she knew. Perhaps even in his death, Ivan could bring people to the Lord. Certainly most of the people in the village had never heard a Christian sermon or seen a Christian funeral. The believers continued to sing until Brother Chapkiy made his way to the front of the coffin, his Bible opened. The last strains of the hymn died out in the still air before he spoke. Quietly, he began. "Blessed in the sight of God is the death of His saints." Several women began to weep softly. Joanna sat down, neither speaking or thinking.

Time seemed to have stopped. She knew that several of the brothers would have preached, especially with so many unbelievers present. And the young people would have read poems. Oddly it seemed that nothing had happened at all, yet they were in the street, making the funeral procession to the cemetery. The glare of the sun almost blinded her as she walked with her husband behind the coffin. Let the world see what had been done to her son! She was glad that the Scripture banners were held high, weaving on their poles in the waves of heat that seemed to rise from the rutted road. Most of the believers had begun a hymn, but Joanna had no heart for singing. The texts had been printed in Moldavian and Russian, and Joanna fixed her gaze on the Moldavian words. "For to me, to live is Christ, and to die is gain." "Do not fear those who kill the body, but are unable to kill the soul." Let there be a witness to the village and the country and to anyone that hears of it that we are not so ignorant that we do not know what has been done! "Seeing on the altar those slain for the Word of God." Let the texts cry out what we cannot speak!

The procession wound slowly along the village road to the cemetery, pulling crowds of workers from the fields and old people from the small farm cottages as it passed. Their son Volodia preceded the coffin, carrying against his chest the large

148

photograph of Ivan that had been taken on his leave. The young face seemed to gaze eloquently at the onlookers as if communicating some profound wisdom. Many from the fields curiously joined the march because the deceased had been after all a young soldier, and this was an unusual funeral. The pastors marched together, singing, the two worn Bibles they had among them carried reverently by Fyodor Gorektoi, the oldest of the pastors, and his cousin, Pyotr. Their white heads and beards glistened in the brilliant summer light.

There was a grove of birch in the corner of the cemetery where the grave had been dug. The long procession formed into a group under the trees, the onlookers squinting curiously in the hot sun. The believers sang "One Sweetly Solemn Thought," and Pastor Chelorskii opened his Bible and preached once more, his eyes returning again and again to the large number of farm workers and old people with small children who listened to his words.

There was something inexorable about the progress of events. Joanna reached suddenly for her husband's arm as the lid with its broken army seals was placed on the coffin and lowered into the earth. The believers were singing "To Our Home Above." Joanna looked painfully over the bent heads of her younger sobbing children to the faces of the young people who had been Vanya's friends. They had carried flowers through the streets and held them in their arms throughout the long service. Now, as shovels of earth thudded onto the coffin top, they slowly moved forward, placing the flowers in heaps around the grave's edge. Stefan Alexandrovich had been carrying the garland-text, "For to me, to live is Christ, and to die is gain." With a thrust he anchored the pole in the grassy earth. The young people moved toward it, kneeling quietly under the banner. A stillness fell upon the crowd. Even the sightseers who had been straining to watch the lowering of the coffin became silent. Under the open sky, on socialist earth, the young people began to pray.

Epilogue

Twelve days after the funeral, the Moiseyevs began telling their story to the world. In a formal protest to Moscow (see following documents), they called for a prompt investigation and an autopsy by a team to include two local Christian doctors.

There was no immediate response. Meanwhile, Ivan's Unit 61968T in Kerch was broken up. The men were reassigned to all parts of the Soviet Union. No two soldiers were left together.

Colonel Malsin's young son fell off a wagon and died as the result of injuries.

Galina Malsin was committed to a psychiatric institution.

Malsin himself was dismissed from his post. He is reportedly distraught and obsessed with the idea that God is punishing him.

The CCECB Council of Prisoners' Relatives immediately gave wide publicity to the martyrdom through its underground bulletins. Letters of condolence from Leningrad to Siberia began to pour into the Moiseyev home. The story soon reached Western news agencies and was published in both secular and religious media in thirty countries, triggering bitter Soviet denials.

Believers passing the story along have been charged and arrested. Two pastors in Sverdlovsk were put on trial, one for simply showing the photo of Ivan's corpse in a church meeting, although he had made no comment about it. Believers report that twenty-two were arrested as far away as Poland.

Russian homes and prayer houses are subject to repeated searches for documents, letters, and tape recordings about Ivan. In parts of Moldavia, overzealous agents ripped the Pentateuch out of believers' Bibles after spotting Moiseyev *(the Russian word for "Moses")* many places throughout the text.

An inquiry commission finally came to Volontirovka in mid-September, 1972, fifty-two days after burial. They began by cross-examining each villager who had signed the funeral document. Each non-Christian, frightened, denied having ever seen the corpse or having said anything about it.

The following day Ivan's body was exhumed. Only his parents and one brother were allowed to observe. The commission, which did not include Christian doctors as requested, excised the heart and surrounding tissue from the body before reburying it.

No commission report has ever been made public.

The last news of Sergei, Ivan's Christian friend, was that he too was undergoing persecution in the closing days of his tour of duty and had been given deadlines to reform.

Another believing Moiseyev son is now in the Red army.

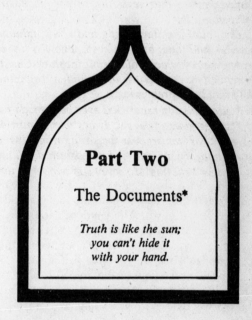

Part Two

The Documents*

*Truth is like the sun;
you can't hide it
with your hand.*

On arriving at my unit, I sought out a place to pray. I noticed one room which was unoccupied until ten A.M. During the day one officer worked there, but no one worked there in the morning until he arrived.

Reveille for soldiers was at six A.M. I dressed and went to this place to pray until breakfast time. The soldiers did their calisthenics and took part in drill, but I prayed two hours. Sometimes I was even late for breakfast because I did not look at my watch.

Thus passed two months. Then came the testing of my faithfulness to the Lord. God showed me how I must act. On that morning, I arose at five and prayed till nine. At about nine I hurriedly went to join the drill formation: everyone was already waiting for me and had looked for me. I had to give an account before the commanding officer for my tardiness. He was already informed that I was a believer. The major ordered me to stand in formation and said that I would be punished. The conversation with him continued in the field.

The soldiers took part in military exercises, but I talked with the officer on another subject. He wanted me to renounce my convictions. When we got back to the barracks, they again summoned me to the commanding officer and there many officers talked with me. They gave me a punishment: Work all night. I worked with joy, singing, and praying. The soldiers took part in drill, but they had me wash the floors in the barracks. The barracks are large. I washed with soap and brush. I was agreeable to everything and rejoiced. The officers noticed this, and as soon as I began to wash, one after another called me in. Finally, I was called to the highest officer—the division commander. But his deputy for political affairs met with me, and I talked with him for about three hours. He first began shouting at me; then he stopped. I asked him, "May I say a few words?" He agreed, thinking that he had already changed my mind and that I would listen to him. But I kept listening to God and not to man. I said to him, "You are shouting for nothing. You can't scare me with your shouting." Then he took two chairs and offered me a seat. Now he talked not as roughly and, finally, convinced that nothing could be done, he left.

After this, I was transferred to another unit, where a colonel talked with me for a whole day.

After twenty days, we completed a 500-kilometer route for drivers, and they sent us to the city of Kerch.

Here they began testing me. The first test was that for five days they gave me nothing to eat. They asked me, "Have you ever been sick?" I told them, "No—I don't know the inside of a hospital." They probably thought that I would get sick during the five days but I did not get sick. The first day went normally, and so on. Glory to God!

I did not get sick because I prayed. They checked with an x-ray examination—I was not sick. They let me go. The officers learned about this and said, "Let him eat, otherwise you'll have us under suspicion if he dies from hunger!"

I did not have to go to drill formation and did not have to sing songs [while marching] with them [during the five days].

Then they tested me another way. It was already wintertime. There was snow outside, and it was thirty degrees below zero Centigrade.* The soldiers slept in the barracks, but they led me out into the street and ordered me to stand out here in the cold for five hours in summer uniform: only a jacket, trousers, boots, and cap. It did not matter to them how I spent the time, only that I stay out on the street for five hours. But I prayed the whole time, however long the stretch was, whether a whole night, one hour, or two hours. Then

---

*—30 degrees Centigrade is equivalent to —22 degrees Fahrenheit.

they summoned me and asked me, "Have you reconsidered or not?" And again the same punishment was repeated. But I did not feel the cold. The officers, when they went out into the street and stood there for ten to twenty minutes, were shaking from the cold. They looked at me and were amazed that nothing had happened to me in such cold weather. At times I stood out for a whole night, even for several nights in a row. This trial lasted for two weeks.

The very first night after the test in the snow, when they had decided to let me sleep in the barracks with the men, I undressed and went to bed after taps at ten o'clock in the evening. I had already gone to sleep, and the soldiers likewise. Suddenly an angel appeared to me and said: "Vanya, get up!" I thought it was a dream. I got up, and I don't remember how I dressed. I flew off with him upwards. We did not fly through the door or window, but the ceiling and the roof of the barracks opened up before us and we flew to another planet.

The angel said to me, "On this planet you will follow behind me, since here you do not have any knowledge of how things are." I consented, and followed after him. We went over a great expanse of grass and arrived at a brook. The angel crossed the brook, but I was afraid. He asked me, "Why do you fear?" "Snakes," I said. "Don't be afraid; you are with me. Here it is not as on the earth. Here there are no snakes."

I crossed over after him. There he showed to me the apostle John. He flew over to me and told me through the angel how life was on this planet. This planet was illuminated better than on earth in the daytime, though I saw no sun anywhere. Next after John, the angel showed me the prophet David. After David, Moses, and then, the prophet Daniel. I did not talk with them. The angel spoke with them and recounted what they said to me.

When we went further, the angel said, "We have traveled a long way and you are tired." We sat under a large tree and rested. The angel told me, "I wish to show you the heavenly city, the new Jerusalem, but if you actually see it as it is, you cannot remain alive. There is still much work for you left on earth. We will fly together to another planet, and I will show you only the light of this city so you will know, while yet alive, that there actually is a new Jerusalem." We flew to the other planet. I saw high mountains. Between the mountains was a deep canyon. The angel lowered me into this canyon and said, "Look upward, and you will see this light." I looked and saw a light brighter than the sun, brighter than the arc of an electric welder. I really thought I would be blinded, but the angel said, "Nothing will happen to you; look." And I looked.

Then the angel said, "The time has come to fly back to earth." We flew back. I remember that the roof and ceiling of the barracks parted and that we landed on the floor. The angel stood on one side of the bed and I on the other. At this instant, the voice of the duty officer resounded, "Reveille." The lights went on, and at this instant the angel disappeared. I looked at my bed all tucked in and at myself. I was dressed. I well remembered everything the angel showed me.

My neighbor from the village of Oloneshta, Suvorovskiy Region in Moldavia, got up and asked, "Where were you during the night?" I answered, "Don't you remember how I got undressed and went to sleep at the same time you did?" He said, "You really did go to bed at the same time I did, but then after three in the morning you disappeared somewhere. Did you actually go into town A.W.O.L.?" I answered, "Let's go and ask the duty officers." The duty officer answered, "No one left during the night. I was standing at the door."

Then I told my neighbor all about the flight with the angel, but he did not believe me. For two days I was in such a condition that I could not understand if I were actually living on earth or not. I worked with my truck correctly, was conscious of everything, but couldn't believe that I was on earth. The rumor about my translation with the angel to heaven went all through the unit. And immediately the officers began working

157

me over. Fifteen to twenty times a day they summoned me to various offices, but I felt victorious, for God was obviously with me.

In January 1971, after being worked over in the military unit in the city of Kerch, they put me into a special rail car for prisoners and sent me to Sverdlovsk. They placed me in a prison in Special Chamber No. 1, from whence they passed me along five special chambers for special tortures.

The first chamber had a cot, where I could lie down.

The second was small, where I could stand and sit on a bench.

The third had a cold nonstop overhead shower, and I could stand.

The fourth was a cold chamber, with the walls of a refrigerator chilled to their limit.

The fifth was a torture chamber for pressure on the body, where they put me in and compressed my entire body by swelling it with air, gradually increasing the air pressure, and every time asking me, "Well then, you better change your mind or else you will be here for seven years." I told them, "If it's God's will, then I will be here seven years, but if not, then tomorrow the torture will stop." This continued for twelve days; afterwards they returned me to Kerch.

They often called me to the headquarters, talked with me, questioned me, and threatened me—all with the aim of re-educating me and preventing me from having free time. If they called me ten times a day, this was not enough. Sometimes they called me fifteen to twenty times a day.

Once our company gathered for a political session. First there were about twenty men assembled. The company commander, who was to conduct the exercise, did not show up for some reason. So the men decided to have their own discussion on the subject of the difference between my God and their god.

They asked me, "Who is your God?" I answered, "My God is almighty and all-powerful." One sergeant, an Armenian from Yerevan, said to me: "If your God is all-powerful and is alive and can do everything, then let Him get me a leave tomorrow to go home. Then I'll believe in Him!" And all the soldiers chimed in, "Yes, if God gives him a leave, then we will know that there actually is a God. But for now, we take everything you're telling us to be a bunch of fairy tales. If, however, your God does it, we will believe that He is a living God and can do anything."

I prayed in my spirit, and the Lord revealed to me, "Tell them that I can do this." Then turning to the sergeant, I said to him, "Tomorrow you will go home on leave, but only if you do what I tell you." He was smoking. "Throw away your cigarette," I said. He threw it away. "And now pull the pack out of your pocket." He got the pack out of his pocket and burned it up.

As this conversation went on, the entire regiment of 150 men gathered. Then our officers arrived and divided us up by jobs. That evening I again met with the sergeant and talked with him all night. I had little sleep, about two hours. He promised that he would believe. I gave some advice to him about how to behave in the village and at home. His parents were unbelievers; they knew nothing about God. And his commander had never even talked about a leave for the sergeant.

The next morning, right after reveille, they sent me out with the truck for some items. Later, I was told that a high-ranking officer had called our regiment from Odessa, some general, and he had ordered that this sergeant be given immediate leave to go home—in ten minutes. I, however, believe that this was not a general but an angel who phoned our regiment. The forms were filled out in the headquarters, and the sergeant took off on his leave. When the men learned about this, they told the officers how we had held a political session yesterday and that everything had "turned out as Vanya had predicted." The officers sent some soldiers chasing after the sergeant to turn him around and thus upset the general opinion of the men that

159

Ivan's God had given the sergeant his leave, but they were too late. The sergeant had already left on the train and they could not catch up with him.

When I got back to our regiment, the men surrounded me and told me joyously that the sergeant had left. I was not able to talk with them, since I was called to headquarters. There the division commander, a major general, waited for me. To his question about what had happened, I told him about everything, starting with yesterday's political session . . . . "But how did you know that he would go on leave?" asked the general. I answered that God had done it.

Evidently, on the general's instructions they wanted to kick me out of this unit and send me somewhere further away, but the men stood up for me. Everyone dropped what he was doing and gathered around the headquarters. Thus I stayed in my unit. After these political sessions, they sent us all to the prairies for harvesting. I wanted to wait for the sergeant to get back from his leave, but they shipped us off to the harvest fields.*

During the time of work in the farmlands, the Lord sent me two visions to confirm my faith. One I saw at night as I came out from my tent. In the beautiful starlit heaven a bright ribbon appeared, but I was unable to read it because of the brightness of the light. I began to read letter by letter like a first-grade boy: "I am coming soon."

Upon our return from harvesting, my unit continued to work in the Odessa province in the village of Zhovtinj, Shirjaevski region. Having finished the work there, our column of vehicles was on its way to the railroad station. I was ordered to get into a truck which had to leave the column and be towed

---

*A letter of Vanya's completes the incident: "When the sergeant got back from leave and I returned from harvesting, a general meeting was held in the unit where I was subjected to jeerings and threats for my preaching. An effort was made to raise up a fuss about the leave, but the sergeant got up and said, 'Whose power was this at work? I now believe that there is a God, for when you rejected my request for a leave, God did a miracle that everyone could see.' There was a lot of rejoicing among the soldiers, but the officers went away shamefaced."

by another truck. Finally my truck completely broke down so that it was impossible even to tow it. The drive shaft had to be removed. I went under the truck and began to remove the drive shaft. None of the soldier drivers thought of putting blocks under the wheels of the truck. And when after much difficulty I succeeded in taking apart the drive shaft, I moved to the side so that it would not fall on me. At that moment the Zil-164, loaded with two tons of earth, moved and its rear wheel came on top of my right shoulder. I just had time to move my head. The wheel stopped on my chest. I began screaming, "Reverse!" Several minutes passed before the driver of the towing truck got the motor started and put it in reverse. They pulled away, and I slid free. I got to my feet, but collapsed right away.

For two hours the entire column stopped on the road while I was coming to consciousness. No medical help of any kind was available. At three o'clock the column arrived at the Zatishye station where there still was no doctor. The superiors, seeing that I was still on my legs, decided to take me in the convoy up to Simferopol, hoping to be there that same day. Meanwhile my arm was already dead. I was breathing with great difficulty.

The army convoy finally came to Simferopol on the third day. We arrived in Simferopol at four in the morning and waited until nine o'clock; then they took me to the army hospital. There the surgeon examined me and told me to raise my arms. The left arm was raised while the right arm remained immovable. The doctor x-rayed the shoulder and arm and put me in a ward. The next day they took me for x-rays again to check my lungs. Again they put me in the ward and told me nothing. During the next twenty-four hours my temperature went up.

The fourth day in the evening—this was November 26, 1971—my temperature went up to forty-two degrees (Centigrade).* I couldn't breathe anymore. My right arm was cold without any feeling. I was able to lie only on my left side.

_____

*107.6 degrees Fahrenheit. Assuming Ivan's memory (or source of information) was accurate, his survival of such a temperature is a miracle in itself.

When supper was served in the ward, I got out of bed and began to pray out loud as if this were my last time on earth. Everyone in the ward heard my prayer. Having prayed, I went to sleep and do not remember anything further.

The following day I woke up at six in the morning and saw that I was lying on my back and both of my arms were raised above my head. I looked at my left arm. I looked at the right—and couldn't believe it . . . I thought this was a dream. Slowly I let down my arms. The right one didn't hurt! I could breathe easily and freely. I took two deep breaths. What is this? I got out of bed and felt the bed. Was it possible that I was sleeping? I did my gymnastics. I breathed freely. Then I began to pray and thank the Lord, but I still could not believe that it was reality. I thought it was a dream, and I laid down to sleep.

During the morning rounds, the doctor on duty came to check. He was told that something had happened to me. He began to take my temperature. I said, "I don't need the thermometer." Then he said, "Take the medicine." "Your medicine will not help," I answered him. He looked at me and was shocked, thinking I had gone out of my mind. "I saw that you could not heal me," I said, "and I turned to my heavenly Physician who healed me during the night." The doctor became even more perplexed. Then I rose and took the thermometer; I was also interested to find out my temperature. It was normal—thirty-seven degrees. The doctor was surprised and went away.

Then the surgeon, a lieutenant colonel by rank, called me to his office and asked, "What happened to you, Moiseyev?" I repeated the same words which I had told the doctor on duty. They had already found out that I was a Christian and understood to which Doctor I had appealed. The surgeon opened the book of records and said, "Look here. This is the kind of treatment we were planning to undertake: to amputate your arm at the shoulder and remove half your lung. Today you were supposed to go through this operation. Now, however, for the first time in my life I see that there truly is a

God and He healed you, because we could have never done anything like this!"

During this conversation in his office, two other doctors were present. I asked if I could return to my unit. He said, "Yes, today I will release you." He wrote everything down in the medical book, gave it to me, and I left.

From the hospital I still had to go to the corps headquarters to get the documents from the farmlands. Near the headquarters were two hundred soldiers who were with me in the farmlands and all of our superiors. Seeing me, they were all amazed. How could this be that after such a heavy trauma I had come out of the hospital in five days?! When I told them what had happened in the hospital, they believed that God exists.

At the corps headquarters I was given papers on which were written my orders, and I went to the bus terminal. I bought a ticket. Suddenly a car pulled up to me. The army chauffeur got out and called me. In the car was a colonel, the head doctor for Crimea. When he found out that the operation had not taken place and that they had released me from the hospital, he became very disturbed. He was told by the doctors about my healing, but he could not believe them and decided to call me back to the hospital. But it was already too late. Briefly I explained to him how the Lord healed me, showed him my arm and my shoulder, and he let me go without a word.

I returned to Kerch to my unit, where many knew me. Once again, many were amazed, having found out about my miraculous healing.

During the time of my trials about which I told earlier, I had another appearance of an angel. When they were endlessly calling me to headquarters for talks with the purpose of reeducation, I would usually pray or sing spiritual hymns on the way. Once on the way from the parking lot to the headquarters I prayed and looked at the sky. It was during dinner time. The sun was shining brightly in the blue sky. Suddenly

163

from the heaven began to descend a bright star which was coming closer and becoming bigger and bigger. And I saw that it was an angel. He came down, not entirely to the ground, but about two hundred meters above the ground and walked in the air above me in the same direction in which my road led. And he said to me, "Ivan, go, don't be afraid, I am with you." So we walked right up to the door of the headquarters; then he became invisible to me. But I firmly believe that he was by my side inside the headquarters when I spoke with the superiors.

About two months ago, or more, before we were sent on a faraway mission, I prayed all night. At three or four in the morning, God, for the comfort of my soul, showed me the heavenly choir which sang the song, "In all the ends of this unhappy earth . . . ." While the angels were singing this song I saw them. They were all in many-colored, bright garments. When they disappeared, the Lord said to me, "This is for the comfort of your soul. Tomorrow you will leave from here." And so it was.

I will read right now from the book of Numbers 22:31. "Then the Lord opened the eyes of Balaam, and he saw the angel of the Lord standing in the way with his drawn sword in his hand; and he bowed all the way to the ground." So today He can also show to all believers His angels and reveal His power. I would also like to read part of the Gospel of Mark—14:35. "And he went a little beyond them, and fell to the ground, and began praying that if it were possible, the hour might pass him by." So, dear brothers, such hours of trouble are times of difficulty and for many of us there are such hours. Jesus Christ prayed then. He knew everything that awaited him beforehand, but we know nothing. I would like to invite you for prayer. As Jesus Christ prayed, so let us kneel down in prayer. *(A prayer follows.)*

Once I was driving a truck loaded with bread. The loaves

had been placed in special trays. The rear doors were fastened with two latches and a padlock. A sergeant accompanying the bread drove with me. Enroute I heard a voice say to me, "Vanya, slow down." This made no sense, so I went on as usual. Again the words were repeated, but for some reason I did not heed them. I looked at my speedometer—it read 60 kilometers an hour.*

Suddenly I saw ahead of the truck a loaf spinning along the asphalt at the same speed as the truck. I was amazed at this miracle and understood at once: God is stopping me. I stopped the truck. I got out with the sergeant and checked the truck. The doors were closed with the same latches and the padlock.

We opened the doors and saw that half the bread was missing. We looked around and saw far behind us our bread lying on the pavement. The sergeant was tremendously amazed at this and said, "Vanya, come here. Tell me, who locked these doors?" "Both of us," I answered. He said, "And all the latches are in place, but the bread has disappeared. I've been with this truck for six years, but this has never happened. The door has two locks so if you slam it hard it locks still better, and besides, there is a padlock. It is impossible for it to open by itself. We closed it, I remember."

"And I remember," I said.

I understood that God had stopped me, for He knew what lay in wait for me ahead. We gathered up the bread and in forty or fifty minutes continued on further. Not far off, at the very first intersection there had been a big accident. An Ikarus bus, which had overtaken us while we were gathering the bread, had smashed into a truck crane. There were fatalities. We would have died in this accident, but God had stopped us. I thanked God, for as He said, "I, God, am your Preserver." And so it was.

We came to the unit. The sergeant told everyone what had happened, but no one believed him. Then they called me into

---

*37 mph.

the office and began interrogating. I explained, "God saved our lives by the miracle with the bread. He loves everyone and is ready to save you as well, even from eternal death awaiting all those who fail to accept Jesus Christ."*

Then the military tribunal had me arrested in the corps headquarters in the city of Simferopol. I was taken to an interrogation before the military prosecutor. There I was told by which article I was going to be judged. The punishment would be from three to seven years. "This is what we have decided," said the prosecutor, "to give you seven years. I give you three days to think it over. If you will not reject your God, you will get seven years."

After questioning they took me to Kerch. Three days passed. They took me to prison. Again they tried to scare me. "This is where you are going to sit." The same day they took me away from there and again gave me a period to think it over for three days. And that period passed.

They came after me and took me to Odessa. There also they wanted to scare me. They ordered me to place my foot in some kind of freezing compartment for five minutes. The foot froze and my boot became white. I couldn't step on this foot since it was completely frozen. I sensed a little bit of pain. Then I began to pray and the foot was healed.

Again they gave me a period to think it over—three days—and took me to Kerch. And this period ran out. Then the prosecutor said, "We are now going to meet in the court." They came after me and said they would take me to Simferopol. They put me on the Simferopol-Irkutsk train, which had a special car for prisoners. They were guarded with automatics. They brought us to Simferopol. I asked when the prosecution would take place. They said, "It is a military tribunal that is going to judge. If there will be a hearing, your

---

*This is the end of the tape made in Moldavia while on leave. The following material from Ivan completes the last weeks of his life.

parents will not come here. Nobody will. And we will sentence you for seven years. So think it over. Where is it better? Two years in the army or seven in the prison?"

I said to let them give me seven years. And they put me in a large prison. The walls were thick—2½ meters*—out of stone. There I sat for ten days. And every day they changed the cell. Of course I was in solitary confinement. For example, in one room there was a bench. One could only stand or sit. In another room there was a bed and one could lie down and it was dry. In a third room water fell from above—cold, real cold! The next room was a refrigerator—cold, cold. One could freeze. And so forth.

They put me in a rubber suit which compresses very hard. They were watching how much a person could stand, so they tried this. "Well, have you been thinking?" they asked. Then they pressed some more, but they saw that a person couldn't stand more, so they let me go. And so it continued ten days. The superiors said, "You will sit here for seven years." I answered, "If it is the will of God that this should be my place, that means I'll be here seven years, but if not, on the second day they will release me from here." After ten days they released me and took me back to Kerch.

---

*Approximately eight feet.

Entries from Vanya's notebook
which he left with believers in Kerch
before his death

In heavy trials day upon day
Be not discouraged as you stand alone,
The call to suffering in this life obey,
Your faraway goal is known.

Advance—fall not back in the terrible storm,
Do not lose heart as you stand alone,
May your heart toward brothers stay ever warm
Advance—fall not back in the storm.

While enemies blaspheme, accuse you, and mock,
Advance—lose not heart in the darkening storm,
Do not lost heart as in deep faith you walk
Sow seeds of righteousness even as they scorn.

Advance alone to the goal,
Harvest comes for men's soul.

I. M.

I must remind myself all of my life how I saw angels for the first time when I was fifteen. Remember, Vanya, how you were working on the earth, and under your feet were snakes, but you continued to walk firmly without fear? You walked a long time until you conquered the biggest snake, and you conquered it because Christ helped you.

Remember the vision when you were standing watch with an angel on a large rock, watching the sea? And a storm came up on the sea, and one ship was going down, and you jumped into the sea on the order of the angel, and you saved many people dragging them to the shore. The waves roared, threatening to sweep you away. When you dragged out the last person, you yourself fell down without strength, but the angel picked you up and put you back on the rock, and there you stood guard again.

Remember how Jesus showed you how much work there is on this earth and how much of the earth is lying without fruit, and that you must cultivate this land?

Remember when you were tired and were going to an interrogation, and an angel, having descended from the sky, said, "Vanya, do not be afraid. Go, I am with you"?

Remember the flaming sign in the sky which said, "I will come soon"? And the announcement written in flame which the Lord forbade you to tell other people about? You are not supposed to tell about this.

Remember when you were in the jail, and they were getting ready to burn you, and how you saw everything?

Remember how for two days you weren't sure whether you were still within the body or without it, after you had seen the heavenly Jerusalem and how much joy it is to live with an angel?

Remember that prayer is the best contact with God.

Remember your family—your father, your mother, brothers, and sisters.

Remember whom you love more—your family or Jesus Christ.

Yet you have not given all of your powers to Christ.

Excerpts from Vanya's last
letters to his parents

Date unknown

Peace to you, my beloved parents. Brothers in Christ from Zaprozhiye spent some time with me. I rejoice, even though someone from a union meeting (AUCECB) betrayed me last week for preaching Christ.

Even though I am a soldier, I work for the Lord, though there are difficulties and testings. Jesus Christ gave the order to proclaim His word in this city, in any meeting, in a military unit, to officers and soldiers. I have been in a division headquarters and in a special section. Though it was not easy, the Lord worked so that it turned out well there. I had an opportunity to proclaim His word to the most senior personnel, but I was reviled and thrown out of the meeting.

Those will be saved who will live not by human will, but by God's will. Observe the commandments of Jesus. You will hear later that I have had many miracles and revelations.

In the Lord,
Your Vanya

June 15, 1972

Christian greetings to my beloved parents. I received your letter and it made me happy. I want to say that by the grace of the love of our gracious Father I am healthy. I wrote you when the Lord revealed to me which is the most correct way and how all Christians must live. In the second letter you will learn about this work, because the Lord has revealed everything.

My dear parents, when I was home, Ilyusha taught me a psalm. I asked you to write it out. Here we see Ilyusha already learning psalms and teaching them to his elders in order for them to sing because they do not know how. Yesterday I was in the Kerch assembly and met there with brethren from another assembly, since we are not associated with the union [AUCECB]. There was a brother from Sochi. And they knew about me. The visit was very good. And everyone here and from Sochi sends greetings in the Lord to all brethren in Moldavia.

My dear parents, the Lord has showed the way to me and I must follow it. And I have decided to follow it. But I do not know if I will return, because the battle is harder than at first. I will now have more severe and bigger battles than I have had till now. But I do not fear them. He goes before me. Do not grieve for me, my dear parents. It is because I love Jesus more than myself. I listen to Him, though my body does fear somewhat or does not wish to go through everything. I do this because I do not value my life as much as I value Him. And I will not await my own will, but I will follow as the Lord leads. He says, "Go," and I go.

Do not become grieved if this is your son's last letter. Because I myself, when I see and hear visions, hear how angels speak and see, I am even amazed and cannot believe that Vanya, your son, talks with angels. He, Vanya, has also had sins and failings, but through sufferings the Lord has wiped them away. And he does not live as he wishes himself, but as the Lord wishes.

Now I want to say a few words to those who do not believe in our Lord Jesus Christ. You call yourselves anti-Christians because you know, though you do not believe, that there is a Lord, who has given me life because this body was dead. You, Semyon, my dear brother, know that the heavenly Father can give you life. Even I have grown very weary with you. Much has passed since then, and I am far from you. But I want you, Semya, to know that there is a God. Know and believe that I have spoken with angels and have flown with them even to another planet where life eternal awaits us. Believe, believe, if you can, all of you who do not yet know Him. I am writing to you because I have seen it all and I know it exists.

June 30, 1972

We greet you all with the great love of Jesus Christ. Your least among the brethren, Vanya, writes you.

I can still write you this letter freely, and you can find out that after my joyous meeting with Sergei, there was not only another storm, but many more. I was glad for everything; when there were no storms, not even adverse winds, then it can become a little tedious. But I am now becoming accustomed to these storms.

Oh, how wonderful and marvelous it is that far from our earth, there is joy! Oh, brethren, keep advancing bravely. Don't be afraid if you have to pass through fire on your way to the heavenly goal.

If your heart will love anything more than Christ, then you are not worthy to follow Him.

Now I want to write to you what kinds of wonderful bodies angels and we will have if we are faithful unto death. I greatly wished to see angels, and I saw them; I saw how they were dressed and told you about them. But their bodies are not like ours; their bodies do not interfere with anyone seeing past them. You can look and see things right through them, as through a glass, and within and without they are pure, pure as crystal, as glass. And everything within can be seen. They have not a single sin, not a single defect. These spiritual bodies we will obtain sometime. With such bodies we can see Jesus Christ and angels, and the heavenly Father; then we will know what one or another is thinking. Oh, what joy, what purity, and what love exists there. How pure everyone is, pure, and even if you polish the best glass, it still remains duller than those bodies awaiting us.

I anxiously await your reply. I wish all of you dear brethren to go forward to this heavenly land.

July 9, 1972

The greetings of your son will soon come to an end. I am weak, but I am still greeting you with the love of Jesus Christ and with the peace of God. They have forbidden me to preach Jesus and I am going through tortures and testings, but I told them that I will not stop bearing the news of Jesus. And the Lord shamed them before the entire unit, when they were torturing me. A soldier stood up who had miraculously gone on leave and had told everyone, and he asked, "Whose power was this?" The authorities did not wish to let me go, and they were put to shame. They then asked me why this tree is green, and the other dry, since the two trees were side by side, one green, the other dry. I asked them what the difference was. They answered, "The difference is great because one is alive and the other is dead." And I told them this is the difference between a believer and an anti-Christian. They still remained nonplussed and greatly embarrassed.

July 11, 1972

I greet you all with the love of Jesus Christ. Vanya writes you this letter. I am very glad for you, and perhaps we can still meet one another. You may have found out that a discharge for me is strictly forbidden. But I am working at full steam for Christ, and I do not want to boast, but I want you to know it, and I hope that you do not forget me in your prayers.

On the tenth of this month, in the evening, I preached Jesus Christ, and after a lengthy discussion one soldier became a believer. I was very glad, and even more strength filled me. There has not yet been a meeting with Sergei.* Glory to the Lord for everything. If I meet with you I will tell you about things in detail, but I cannot write about them in a letter.

> When he sees how the sea rages
> For those returning from the fray,
> > "Fearsome waves over us roll,
> > Joy and courage fills our soul."

---

*Evidently this is in addition to the "joyous meeting" with Sergei mentioned in the June 30 letter.

For those who from the fearsome, pressing waves
Returned with victory to the shore,
 "We move onward toward the shore,
 We move to victory evermore.

 For you will be days without dawn again,
 As a soldier, the anguish of separation's pain
 Nor easy months in depths most troubling,
 Hearing, it seems, the groans of brothers doubling."

But no! Might abundant sends the Lord
In their example hope upon him is poured
Whatever sternness his lot affords.

He does fulfill heaven's most difficult order
His last strength he shares with another
Oft struggling with the sea's raging weather.

What he does he is ordered to do
Though it is hard for him to go through
He obeys Christ's sacred command!

I feel that you will not see me any longer, . . . and if you think about coming to me, it is useless. I will not forget you in prayer. I very earnestly wish to meet with Sergei. Perhaps, my last work has already been done. Receive my heartfelt Christian greetings from the least of the brethren. I do not await your answer and I ask you not to write.

Till we see one another, God be with you, dear friends. I have become sad thinking about you, but one thing I remember: I go fulfilling Christ's orders . . . .

Greetings from Vanya

July 14, 1972

The work is great, and I follow Jesus' command. The testings are great and the sufferings are not light. I have much to write that I cannot write in letters. I am awaiting the visit from Sergei as the Lord promised. Oh, that we may not now be ashamed of speaking about the Lord. All have seen the miracles and say that in truth God exists. I will plant seed and will move ahead, as the Lord teaches me through the Holy Spirit and the angels.

Don't be offended, but I am striving in this work. Also know that it is not easy for the body. Now I go to meetings, though they have forbidden it. The brothers send greetings to all. And I send greetings to all: Slabodzeya and Yernokley [village ECB churches].

I wish that Semya and Galya could believe in and see the power of the Lord to see that He exists, just as all do here: officers and soldiers say that there is a God and fear Him, for they see miracles and His might. I also wish that grandmother could believe and that she would know that the path she is following leads to hell. Jesus Christ is still calling you and He would give you life eternal, but I cannot give life. Believe in the gospel. If you hear that I am not at liberty, then know that here in the city of Kerch I have left a notebook where I have described the miracles, and maybe you can come, or they can bring it to you; the Lord knows all. Be true Christians. He will fortify you and send you His strength.

Ask, for He is rich in all, and all that you wish He gives free.

I do not forget you in my prayers.

In the Lord, Vanya

July 15, 1972 (to his brother, Vladimir)

Dear brother, I received your letter and am late in answering you because there was a great storm. When Sergei came, even he got it, and his literature and even post cards were confiscated.

Don't tell our parents everything. Just tell them, "Vanya wrote me a letter and writes that Jesus Christ is going into battle. This is a Christian battle, and he doesn't know whether he will be back."

I desire that all of you, dear friends, young and old,

175

remember this one verse. Revelation 2:10—"Be faithful unto death, and I will give you the crown of life."

Receive this, the last letter on this earth, from the least of the brethren.

Vanya

The funeral document

Акт

Мы нижеподписавшиеся являемся
свидетелями в том, что привезённый
труп Моисеева Ивана Васильевича
1952 г. рождения с военной службы
в г. Керчь в/ч 61968 "П" не подтверждается
свидетельством о смерти № 286064 1-А.Б.
диагнозом "Механическая асфиксия
от утопления", но утверждаем, что
смерть постигла в результате
умышленного насилия. Подтверждаем
снимками и фактами: Сердце проколото шесть
раз, нои и голова сильно побиты, на груди ожог.

Свидетели тела Володинировки подписались:

1. Моисеев В. Т.   Моисеев
2. Моисеева И. К.   Моисеева
3. Моисеев В. В.   [подпись]
4. Моисеев В. С.   [подпись]
5. Моисеева Н. В.   Моисеева
6. Голюк С. П.   [подпись]
7. Алду С. И.   [подпись]
8. Гросскович М. И.   Гросскович
9. Изману В. С.   [подпись]
10. Слюсаренко А. С.   Слюсаренко
11. Туйёску В. Г.   Туй
12. Каскарь П. И.   Каскарь
13. Алсу А. Ф.   Алсу
14. Ефимова А. И.   Ефимов
15. Молкош Е. Е.   Молкош
16. Ефимова А. Ч.   Ефимова
17. Ефимова А. С.   Ефимова
18. кошельник А. Ф.   Кошельник
19. Шорова И. И.   Шорова
20. Тэлмицкая А. М.   Тэлмицкая
21. Колисниченков И.   [подпись]
                          [подпись]

22. Тэлма П. А.   Тэлма
23. Тэлма Е. С.   Тэлма

STATEMENT

July 19-20, 1972

We, the undersigned, are witnesses to the fact that the corpse of Moiseyev, Ivan Vasilievich, born 1952, brought home from military service in the city of Kerch, military unit 61968T, did not correspond to the Death Certificate No. 2860641-AT giving the diagnosis of "Mechanical aphyxiation due to drowning," but we state that death occurred as a result of premeditated violence. We confirm this with photographs and facts: the heart was punctured six times, the legs and the head were severely beaten, and there were burns on the chest.

Witnesses—residents of Volontirovka village

1. Moiseyev, V. T.   /signature/
2. Moiseyeva, J.C.   "
3. Moiseyev, V. V.   "
4. Moiseyev, S. V.   "
5. Moiseyeva, I. V.   "
6. Chapkiy, S. P.   "
7. Albu, S. I.   "
8. Prokopovich, M. M.   "
9. Romonu, D. Ye.   "
10. Slyusarenko, A. S.   "
11. Butesku, V. G.   "
12. Paskar, T. M.   "
13. Albu, M. F.   "
14. Yefremova, A. I.   "
15. Mankosh, Ye. Ye.   "
16. Yefremov, Ya. V.   "
17. Yefremova, A. S.   "
18. Kotelnik, A. F.   "
19. Blomitskaya, A. M.   "
20. Shorova, I. I.   "
21. Kolisniczenko, Ye. I.   "

22. Toma, T. A.   "
23. Toma, Ye. S.   "

Ivan's body on July 20, 1972.

Seated: Vasiliy and Joanna Moiseyev and their three younger sons. Directly behind Joanna is a Moiseyev daughter; the other three girls are her friends. *The back row, l. to r.:* Roman, Semyon, another friend, and Vladimir. This photo was taken sometime after Ivan's death.

The open letter from Vanya's church

> "And others were tortured, not accepting their release, in order that they might obtain a better resurrection."
>
> Hebrews 11:35
>
> "My faithful martyr . . . was slain . . . ."
>
> Revelation 2:13

OPEN LETTER
TO ALL CHILDREN OF GOD COMPRISING THE CHURCH
OF OUR LORD JESUS CHRIST

Beloved brothers and sisters in the Lord! We report to you a sorrowful event. This grief is our common grief, for we all comprise a single Church, the single Body of Christ.

On July 17, 1972, Brother Moiseyev, Vasiliy Trofimovich, and his wife Joanna Constantinova received an urgent telegram from the city of Kerch, military unit 61968T: "Your son, Moiseyev, Ivan Vasilievich, has died tragically." In turning over the body to the relatives, a death certificate was given, stating in the Cause of Death column "Mechanical asphyxiation from drowning." In the expert's statement from the autopsy it is specified: "Death occurred due to violence." Before interment, the coffin was opened and the body inspected, and all were horror-stricken. There were six deep punctures in the area of the heart; the left and right sides of the head bore wounds and abrasions; the feet and back were severely beaten; there were large burns on the chest so that the rapping of a finger along the chest could be heard. There were black and blue marks around the mouth.

Knowing Vanya to be a faithful witness of Christ, we declare:

He was tormented and tortured for Jesus. July 16 of this year was the date of the final deadline for Ivan to reconsider the consequences of his faith. "Persons in civilian dress" (thus states documented testimony) with the participation of military commanders repeatedly gave I. Moiseyev "deadlines to ponder" with the demand that he renounce his Christian convictions. He suffered and was tortured but remained faithful to God; his torturers did not hear any rejection of his faith. Then, while still alive, he was forcibly drowned in the sea at a depth of 156 cm. in order to hide the traces. Vanya's height was 185 cm.*

We have experienced profound grief at the sight of his parents sobbing at his coffin and recognizing the face of their son only with great difficulty. But we consoled them and ourselves by the fact that we all have a heavenly Father, a Comforter, and a righteous Judge.

There were many people at the coffin of the martyred brother: brothers, sisters, local people, and people from other points, who took part in a reverential service to the Lord. The funeral service took place on July 20, 1972, in the afternoon with the singing of hymns and the carrying of garland-texts in the Moldavian and Russian languages: "For to me, to live is Christ, and to die is gain," "Do not fear those who kill the body, but are unable to kill the soul," and "Seeing on the altar those slain for the Word of God."

This is the face of the godless; they add to the measure of their lawlessness, to which is borne witness by this martyr's end of dear Brother Moiseyev, Ivan Vasilievich.

On giving to the earth the remains of martyred Brother Vanya, we returned to our places with reverence and the desire

---

*Their contention is that the water at the stated place is only 5' 1½" deep. Ivan, being 6' 1", could hardly have drowned in such shallow water unless he were held down or were unconscious.

to serve more zealously the Lord and, just as Brother Vanya, to be faithful to Him until death.

Yes, even in our day the unheard-of is being done; pay heed to what we advise and say. Tell this to all people who love the Lord, tell about this to all, both great and small, so that all who fear the Lord and who await His returning may call in one spirit and one accord to the Lord, defending and standing fast for the truth.

Be steadfastly faithful, faint not in the way,
The Lord will strengthen your spirit and scatter the gloom
And the sun will yet warm you with its faithful rays,
The dark path He will dawn on anew.

Let black storm clouds cover heaven's deep blue
And the sun no more shine on your way,
Forget not that Almighty God is with you
Faint not but in joy advance to the day.

I.M. Moiseyev

> Your brothers and sisters from the Slobodzeyskaya, Yermokleyskaya, Zamiskaya, Benderovskaya, and Tiraspolskaya churches, participants in the funeral ceremony of July 20, 1972, Volontirovka village. (*68 names follow.*)

The Moiseyevs' formal protest to the world

To: A. A. Grechko, Minister of the Armed
    Forces of the USSR
    L. I. Brezhnev, General Secretary of the
    Central Committee of the CPSU
    K. Waldheim, General Secretary of the
    UN
    International Committee for the Defense
    of Human Rights at the United Nations
    Professor M. V. Keldysh, President
    of the USSR Academy of Sciences
    Chairman of the Union of Writers of
    the USSR
    Editors of the Newspapers:
      Sovetskaya Rossiya
      Pravda
      Izvestiya
    Council of Churches of ECB in the USSR
    Council of ECB Prisoners' Relatives
    in the USSR (CPR)*
    To all Christians

From: *The Parents of Moiseyev, Ivan Vasilie-
    vich*
    Killed during torture for his faith in God
    in the ranks of the Soviet Army, a resi-
    dent of Volontirovka Village, Suvorovskiy
    Region, Moldavian SSR

    "And it came about that all who saw it
    said, 'Nothing like this has ever happened
    . . . to this day.' "   Judges 19:30

EXTRAORDINARY REPORT

On July 16, 1972, our son and brother Moiseyev, Ivan
Vasilievich, born 1952, died for the convictions of his faith in

---

*The Council of Evangelical Christian/Baptist Prisoners' Relatives in the USSR
(CPR) was formed by members of the CCECB in 1961 for the defense of men and
women imprisoned because of their Christian beliefs.

God from terrible martyr's torments in the city of Kerch while in service in the Soviet Army (Military Unit 61968 "T").

Covered with wounds, haggard from torture, but still alive, in the presence of Lieutenant Colonel Malsin, V.I., he was forcibly drowned in the Black Sea at a depth of 156 cm. while his height was 185 cm.

The death certificate cited "Mechanical asphyxiation from drowning." The autopsy analysis read: "Death followed as the result of violence."

On July 17, 1972, at eight A.M. , we received a telegram: "Your son has died tragically. Please inform us of your arrival." On arriving in the city of Kerch, we decided to inter him in his native village. We were shown the face of our son in the coffin, after which the same coffin was soldered shut. With us was our son Semyon, a Komsomol member, whom the military unit commander summoned individually into his office and talked to him about something for a long time, about which our Semyon told us not a word.

For participation in the funeral ceremony and delivery of the coffin to Volontirovka village, from the military unit were sent Captain Platonov, V.V., also an extended-service sergeant, and a private, who brought the coffin to the village on July 20, 1972. On receiving the coffin bearing the body of our son, we decided to inspect the body and to photograph it. To do this, we began to break the welds of the coffin lid.

Platonov, V.V., and the sergeant seated nearby us, became alarmed on seeing this and immediately announced, "We have to go, we're in a hurry," and quickly got into the vehicle and disappeared. On opening the coffin, we began to remove clothing to inspect the body, but Semyon, using physical force, did not allow us to inspect the body and to photograph it, declaring to all his relatives, "Photograph him dressed." Those present saw the following marks on the body: in the area of the heart six deep punctures with a round object, on the head abrasion wounds to the left and to the right, the legs and back were severely beaten, large burns on the chest so that rapping with a finger along the skin was audible, and bruises around the mouth. All this was confirmed by twenty-three witnesses, residents of Volontirovka village, by a statement dated July 20, 1972 (we attach the statement).

From the testimony of the unit commander Malsin, V.V., in a conversation with us, Vanya's parents, the following must be noted: "On the morning of the sixteenth I was occupied and had a conversation in the unit with a group of governmental guests. In the afternoon I drove with Moiseyev to the beach in a GAZ-69 truck." In the words of soldier eyewitnesses, Malsin drove in a Pobeda car together with unknown civilians, and Moiseyev followed after them alone in the GAZ-69 truck in an unknown direction.

On July 19, 1972, in handing over Moiseyev's body, Malsin stated: "Moiseyev died hard, he fought with death, but he died a Christian. Today I am smoking my seventh pack of cigarettes." On August 1 of this year he said, "My wife lost nine pounds in a week from the experiences of Moiseyev's death," declaring that "She no longer will ride in the vehicle he drove."

(Next follows excerpts from Ivan's tape recording and letters to document his persecution while in the army.)

We wish again to repeat the words of Lieutenant Colonel Malsin, V. I.: "Moiseyev died hard; he fought with death, but he died a Christian."

WE, THE PARENTS, ASK THAT:

1. A medical experts' commission be sent at once to autopsy and establish the cause of death of the tormented body of our son.
2. An investigation be made to find and convict the criminals who tortured him.

3. We Christian parents have four other sons younger than Ivan who face service in the army, but until the murderers are found and charged and a necessary guarantee of the safety of our believing children in the army is given, we will not hand over our four sons to serve in the same.

4. Considering that believers in our country have been subjected to undeserved insults and slander, and many incidents of the victims have been deliberately distorted, we believe that the experts' commission will be incompetent without the participation of a doctor from among Christians. Therefore we will give our agreement to autopsy the body of our son Ivan only in the presence of our relatives and two doctors from among believers, whom we will present on the day that this commission arrives. We request that its arrival be announced to us four days in advance.

We attach to this report the following:

1. Statement of witnesses.
2. Copy of the death certificate.
3. We will present the photographs of the body areas to the commission of experts at the time the body is autopsied.

Respectfully: (signatures) Moiseyev, V. T.
Moiseyeva, J. C.
Moiseyev, V. V.
Moiseyev, R. V.
Moiseyeva, M. V.

Please reply to: Moldavian SSR
Suvorovskiy Region
Volontirovka Village

August 1, 1972

The Moiseyevs' appeal to their national church leadership in Moscow

To: The Council of ECB Churches in the
USSR
The Council of ECB Prisoners'
Relatives in the USSR

From: Moiseyev, Vasiliy Trofimovich,
Moiseyeva, Joanna Constantinova
residents of Volontirovka village,
Suvorovskiy Region, Moldavian
SSR

"I saw underneath the altar the souls of
those who had been slain because of the
word of God, and because of the testimony
which they had maintained. . . . And there
was given to each of them a white robe; and
they were told that they should rest a little
while longer, until the number of their
fellow-servants and their brethren who
were to be killed even as they had been,
should be completed also."

Revelation 6:9,11

REPORT

Dear brothers and sisters:

We are compelled to add to your continuing sorrow for the
sake of Jesus Christ. Our son, Moiseyev, Ivan Vasilievich, born
1952, a member of the Slobodzeya ECB Church, performing
military service in the city of Kerch . . . received a martyr's death
on July 16, 1972 for the witness of Jesus Christ. Beaten,

wounded, burned with a red-hot iron, but yet alive, he was drowned in the Black Sea at a depth of 156 cm., while his height was 185 cm.

"Death occurred as a consequence of violence." Thus reads the expert's report from his autopsy.

Our son has added to the number of those slain for God's Word. Along with our grief, we rejoice for his exploits of suffering. He, more than anything else in the world, loved Jesus during his life and proved this.

In his last letters he often reminded us, "If you love anything or anyone in this world more than Jesus, you cannot follow Him" .... Looking unto the blessed Teacher, he believed steadfastly and suffered.

Let this living flower, having given the fragrance of its youth on the cross, serve as a good example for all Christian youth to so love Christ as our son Vanya loved Him.

... We ask you to report through the bulletin that testings have reached us, but God is faithful, who will help us to overcome them.

Vanya's relatives: father, mother, brothers, and sister
August 1, 1972

BULLETIN
of the Council of Evangelical Christian/Baptist Prisoners'
Relatives in the USSR

> "Remember the prisoners, as though
> in prison with them; and those who are
> ill-treated, since you yourselves also
> are in the body."   Hebrews 13:3

Moscow, 1972

Dear brothers and sisters!

"Precious in the sight of the Lord is the death of His godly
ones" and even more precious is the martyr's death of faithful
witnesses of Christ.

Much material (documents, photographs, letters, tape recordings, and eyewitness testimony) about the martyr's death of a
Christian youth, our dear brother Ivan Moiseyev, has arrived
at the Council of Evangelical Christian/Baptist Prisoners'
Relatives.

With deep sorrow we report to you about this flagrant case
of lawlessness and arbitrary actions, which has been repeated
not in the Barnaul Prison, as formerly with Brother Nikolai
Khmara in 1964, but in the Soviet army. But the hands of the
secret butcher-executioners, as documents testify, are in both
cases the same.

This information is not intended to excite wrath or indignation against the persecutors of Christ's church in our
country and their subordinate atheists, but, first of all, to call

them to repentance (Psalm 2:10-12) and to take heed that if they do not repent, then they will inevitably stand before the righteous Judge, who will require of them all the righteous blood spilled in our country and will pay them according to their deeds, as stated in Matthew 23:32-33, 35.

Secondly, the Council of Prisoners' Relatives, together with the parents of Brother Vanya Moiseyev, desire and pray that the Lord through this martyr's death will stir up many children of God and all Christian youth and inspire them for an even more selfless witness to a perishing world about salvation in Christ.

Jesus Christ, crucified again even through this glorious death, conquered the world and conquered our persecutors! They can wash away their shame only with tears of deep repentance and with Christ's blood.

May the spiritual eyes of many Christians be opened to see this triumph, and may many be filled with His Holy Spirit for good exploits in the cause of evangelism.

Let Christ's love
In our hearts burn
As the lighthouse beacon glows
That friends and foes
May always learn
How great is Christ Jesus' love.

I.M. (from his notebook)

Council of ECB Prisoners' Relatives in the USSR

Press "Explanations" of Ivan's Death

January 5, 1973

Wire service release
which appeared in many Russian newspapers

On a hot July day in 1972 a soldier named Ivan Moiseyev drowned approximately a hundred meters from shore at Cape Borzovka near the city of Kerch. Many were in the water with him, so the chap was quickly dragged to the shore. Everything was done to save him. At first artificial respiration was administered. Later, after the indirect massage of the heart, Dr. E. Novikovo injected adrenalin into the heart and ofedrin into a vein. However, the struggle for life was in vain, and the following autopsy showed that he was drowned, with paralysis of the heart following immediately.

The death of the young man was taken very hard by his comrades in the service, but it would never enter their minds that this unfortunate accident would be used by base people who counted Ivan as their "brother." Among his relatives there turned out to be Evangelical Christians/Baptists. The leaders of the Council of Churches of Evangelical Christians/Baptists decided to use the death of their "brother" to achieve a provocation. They told those who gathered at Moiseyev's funeral in the village of Volontirovka [Moldavia] that Ivan was "tortured." The marks on his body were from the attempts to save his life and from the autopsy, but they were falsely interpreted as evidences of horrible tortures. At the funeral the provokers obtained a collection of signatures under a slanderous "document."

June 9, 1973 *Altajka Pravda*
Account allegedly by Semyon Moiseyev, Ivan's brother

НЕ МОГУ МОЛЧАТЬ

Моего брата нет в живых. Не хочется верить в такое. Ведь ему исполнилось только двадцать, когда нелепая смерть оборвала его жизнь. Для меня он всегда был и остается родным. Мы выросли под одним кровом, нас ласкали руки одной матери. И учились в одной школе в селе Волонтировка Суворовского района. Жалею об одном. Я разорвал путы, которыми нас с детства связали по рукам и ногам баптисты, а Ване этого сделать не удалось...

Его не стало. Так называемые «братья во Христе» подняли вой чуть ли не на весь мир, утверждая, что Ваня пострадал за веру, что его насильно утопили. Не могу молчать, когда кое-что плетет всякую чепуху, замахивается на наши советские порядки, бросает тень на советских людей. Вы лжете, вы порочите память моего доброго брата, моих отца и мать. У нас с ним были разные взгляды на мир. Он оставался верующим, а я уже нет. Но различия во взглядах не сделали нас врагами. Мы иногда спорили. Я знал, что еще немного, и мой брат порвет с баптистами. Мне было больно, когда узнал, что случилось несчастье. Вместе с родными я выехал в Керчь, чтобы забрать его тело и предать земле на родине...

Спустя 10—15 дней так называемый «совет церквей евангельских христиан-баптистов» сочинил фальшивку на смерть брата. Я читал этот их бюллетень. В нем сплошные бредни. Вы только послушайте. Утверждается, что Ваню преследовали за веру, наказывали, лишали увольнений в город, подвергали пыткам и т. д. Клевета это!

Будучи в части, где служил брат, я разговаривал с его командирами, солдатами. Никто не сказал плохого слова о Ване. Он был исполнительным солдатом, являлся шофером командира части. За год службы имел семь благодарностей командования. Два раза ему предоставляли краткосрочный отпуск домой. Баптисты уверяют, что Ваню притесняли. Неправда! Я сам служил в Советской Армии и знаю, что там нет гонений на солдат, которые исповедуют ту или иную религию. Ваня тоже имел возможность отправлять обряды. Ведь ему, как и другим, давались увольнительные. В это время он мог посещать и посещал молитвенный дом.

Баптисты пытаются утверждать, что мой брат был замучен и утоплен. Ложь! Разговаривал я с теми, кто присутствовал при этом несчастном случае. Утонул он случайно. От этого никто не гарантирован. На его теле действительно были пятна. Но не от пыток и раскаленного железа, как уверяют баптисты. Это следы массажа, уколов, когда люди делали все возможное, чтобы спасти Ваню.

Мы привезли труп брата домой в цинковом гробу. И вот тут-то я понял, что вожаки баптистов что-то замышляют. Они решили сфотографировать труп. Я, конечно, противился. Меня силой оттолкнули от гроба: ведь их в доме было много. Во время похорон одураченным односельчанам баптисты подсовывали подписаться на чистом листе бумаги. Люди шли на это. Они не думали, что потом выше их подписей главари баптистов состряпают «акт», в котором утверждают, что смерть Вани наступила «в результате умышленного насилия...». Какая бессовестная подделка!

Чьих рук это дело? Так называемых баптистов - раскольников и их руководителей прежде всего. Об этих нелегальных «братьях» Ваня знал, встречался с ними, но правды им не говорил. Что это так, приведу такой пример. Во время своего второго отпуска Ваня всем нам, в том числе дяде Веребчану, говорил, что службой доволен. Военную присягу давно принял (замечу, что баптисты-раскольники зачастую отказываются от ее принятия). Днем же позже, встречаясь с этими нелегальными «слугами господними» в Тирасполе, он не сказал им, что принял присягу. Вводил их в заблуждение.

Вожаки евангельских христиан-баптистов от имени моих родителей сочинили письмо, содержащее клевету на честных людей. Зачем это они сделали! Да, мои родители верующие. Но они никогда не встанут на грязный путь, чтобы клеветать на советских людей, на наши порядки. Они знают, что Советская власть открыла им и их детям путь к счастливой жизни. И если в нашей семье случилось горе, то не пытайтесь на нем погреть руки. Не выйдет! Мы отметаем вашу клевету! Не ворошите своими грязными руками светлую для нашей семьи память сына и брата Вани.

Ваш бюллетень — фальшивка. Он нужен в интересах тех, кто вами, вожаки христиан-баптистов, повелевает из-за рубежа. Мне, например, известно, что клеветническая информация о гибели Ивана Моисеева была переведена на многие языки, размножена и распространяется по 15 странам. Так вот, оказывается, почему вы стали такими прыткими. Но помните, советских людей не обмануть.

Семен МОИСЕЕВ,
рулевой моторист Бендерского эксплуатационного участка управления речного транспорта.
Молдавская ССР.

I CANNOT BE SILENT

My brother is dead. It is hard to believe it. For he was only twenty years old when the senseless death cut off his life. To me he has always been and still is very dear.

We grew up under the same shelter; we were both caressed by the gentle hands of our mother. We went to the same school in the village of Volontirovka, Suvorovskiy district. I regret one thing. I broke the chains with which the Baptists bound our hands and feet, but Ivan did not.

He is gone. The so-called brothers in Christ set up a wail nearly through the entire world, maintaining that Ivan suffered for the cause of his belief, that he was drowned by force. I cannot be silent, when some people talk all kind of nonsense, threaten our Soviet rules, and throw shadows on the Soviet people. You tell lies, you malign the remembrance about my brother, you malign my mother and my father. He and I had different opinions about the world. He remained a believer, and I not. However, the difference in opinion did not make us enemies. We argued at times. I thought that it would not be long and my brother would break up with the Baptists. I was grieved when I learned that Ivan had a misfortune. The family and I went to Kerch to get his body and bury him in the homeland.

Ten or fifteen days later, the so-called Council of Churches of Evangelical Christians/Baptists composed a fake document about my brother's death. I read that bulletin. It contained sheer nonsense. Just listen to it. "It has been affirmed that Ivan was persecuted for his faith, he was punished, he was deprived of free time to go to the town, he was tortured, etc." All that is a slander.

I was honored to be where my brother served in the army. I conversed with his commanders and with the soldiers. They had nothing against him. He carried out his duties faithfully, he was the chauffeur of the commander of the military unit where he served in the military service. Within one year of military service he had seven merit points from his commander. He was twice offered short-term leave home. The Baptists try to persuade that Ivan was oppressed in the army. It is not true. I have been in military service myself, and I know that the soldiers are not persecuted, even those who profess religious faith. Ivan had an opportunity to exercise religious ceremonies. For he, like the other soldiers, received passes. On his free time he could go, and he attended prayer meetings.

The Baptists try to contend that my brother was martyred and later drowned. It is an outrageous lie! I talked to those who were present at the accident. He drowned by accident. It can happen to anybody. Indeed there were marks on his body, but not from torture or scorching iron as the Baptists assure it was. Those marks were signs from the massages and shots, when people applied all means to save Ivan.

We brought my brother's body home in a coffin made of zinc. Here I understood that the Baptists' leaders were plotting something. They decided to take pictures. They pushed me aside from the coffin; there were many of them in the house. At the funeral, the Baptists pushed a blank sheet of paper to the fool countrymen to sign their names on it. People agreed to do it. They did so without thinking that later, above their names, the Baptists' leaders would compose an "act" in which they maintain that Ivan's death was caused as a result of premeditated murder. What a dishonest counterfeit!

Who did it? So-called Baptists and, above all, their leaders. Ivan knew about those illegal brothers; he met with them; however, he did not tell them the truth. On his second leave, he told to all of us, including Uncle Verebtchany, that he was content with the military service. He had taken the military oath a long time ago. (I should say that the Baptists very often refuse to take the military oath.) A day later, after he took the oath, he met with the illegal servants of God in Tiraspole; he did not tell them that he had taken the oath. He misled them.

The leaders of the Evangelical Christian/Baptist church composed the letter on behalf of my parents, which accused honest people. Why did you do that? Yes, my parents are Christian, but they will never get involved in dirty business; they will never slander our people or our governmental system. They know that the Soviet regime opened up a door for them and their children to a happier life. And if in our family misfortune took place, then do not try to take advantage of it. It will not work! We swept aside your slander! Do not erase, with your dirty hands, the respectful memory of a son and brother Ivan.

Your bulletin is a fraud. It is needed by the leaders of the Christian/Baptists who gave you orders from abroad. I know, for example, that the slanderous information about Ivan Moiseyev's death was translated into many languages, multiplied, and spread into fifteen countries.

Thus it was found out why you were so quick. Remember, however, you cannot fool Soviet people.

Moldavian SSR

Semyon Moiseyev,
truck driver

June 9, 1973 *Altajka Pravda*
Account by an alleged eyewitness

Я ЗНАЮ ПРАВДУ

Волею обстоятельств я видела, как на самом деле погиб Иван Моисеев, знаю всю правду о его смерти.

Поверьте, мне, как и всем знавшим об этой трагической истории, трудно вспоминать о ней. Во цвете лет, нежданно-негаданно погиб молодой человек, которому бы еще жить и жить. У кого не сожмется сердце от горя! Но необходимость дать отпор клеветникам, рассказать обманутым ими людям всю правду заставляет меня вновь вернуться к событиям июля прошлого года.

Мы решили погостить несколько дней у моей двоюродной сестры Ларисы. Утром Владимир — ее муж, офицер Советской Армии, хотел показать нам достопримечательности Крыма. Наша машина сломалась, и, пока ее ремонтировали, Владимир договорился, чтобы нам дали автомобиль. На нем мы поехали в Керчь. За рулем его сидел молоденький солдат. Потом я узнала, что это был Иван Моисеев.

Стало очень жарко, и мы решили искупаться, поехали к мысу Борзовка. Владимир сказал детям и шоферу:

— Только не спешите сразу в воду. Остынете, тогда уж купайтесь.

Потом добавил для Ивана:

— А ты только окунись и сразу к машине. Скоро дальше поедем.

Пошли они купаться, а я осталась. Сижу, с людьми разговариваю. Вдруг бежит Лариса, кричит:

— Шофер наш пропал!
— Как пропал!

— Смотри!

Вижу — Владимир плавает, ищет, а с берега кричат ему, показывают, где Иван в воду погрузился. Потом те, кто стоял на берегу, рассказывали, что Моисеев вынырнул, что-то крикнул и снова ушел под воду.

Минут десять прошло. Владимир все искал Моисеева. Но тут волна вынесла его тело. Люди сразу подхватили его, давай откачивать. Меня послали вызвать «скорую помощь». Неподалеку не то интернат, не то дом отдыха был. Вызвала «скорую», и пока со мной на берег поехал тамошний врач.

Врач стал делать искусственное дыхание. Потом он говорит: «Спирт нужен. А где его взять?» Кинулись к палаткам на берегу, там туристы жили. У них нашелся спирт.

Кто-то кричит врачу: «Говорите, что еще нужно, все найдем. Лишь бы парень жив остался!»

Но и растирание спиртом не помогло. Врач говорит:

— Горчичники нужны.

Нашли в палатках и горчицу.

Тут и «скорая помощь» приехала. Сделали Моисееву инъекцию. Через некоторое время еще одна машина «скорой помощи» примчалась. Опять укол сделали, опять искусственное дыхание...

Три часа бились за жизнь Ивана, но все оказалось бесполезным. Человек пятьдесят собралось около его тела. И все они, горько переживая смерть солдата, плакали...

И вдруг теперь я узнаю, что нашлись клеветники, которые даже такое тяжелое горе хотят использовать в своих провокационных целях. Что следы, оставшиеся от попыток спасти Моисеева, от медицинской экспертизы, они объявляют свидетельствами «пыток». Каким же бессовестным, циничным надо быть, чтобы осмелиться на такое!

Я знаю, откуда тянется эта клевета. Я была в части, куда родственники Ивана приехали, чтобы забрать его тело. Один из них, едва взглянув на покойного, даже не отдав положенной дани скорби, стал твердить: «Я знаю, его убили, вы его замучили. Мне даже показалось, что он приехал уже с готовой версией и только искал все, что может лишь как-то ее «подтвердить».

О какой же святости, любви к ближнему могут твердить вожаки евангельских христиан-баптистов, если у них нет и простой человеческой совести! К служению каким же «высоким идеалам веры» могут они звать своих единоверцев!

Нас было человек пятьдесят, видевших смерть Ивана Моисеева. И если люди, объявившие его своим «братом», спекулируют на его гибели, если они продали свою совесть за тридцать импортных сребреников, то мы не позволим им греть руки на несчастье других, за грязной клеветой прятать свои черные души.

Л. А. МАРТЫНЕНКО,
жительница г. Ставрополя.

I KNOW THE TRUTH

Due to the circumstances, I personally witnessed how Ivan Moiseyev perished. I know the whole truth about his death.

Believe me, for us who know the tragic story, it is hard to talk about it. In the full bloom of life, a young man unexpectedly perished; he would have still lived a full life. Whose heart will not wring from grief! However, the necessity to refute the slanderers and to tell the whole truth to those who were deceived by the slanderers forces me to come back to the event which took place in July of last year.

We decided to spend a few days with my cousin, Larisa. Early in the morning Vladimir, her husband, a Soviet military officer, wanted to show us the sights of the Crimea. Our automobile broke down, and while it was being repaired, Vladimir made arrangements for us to get a military car. We drove to Kerch. The driver was a young soldier. Later I found out that the young soldier was Ivan Moiseyev.

It became very hot and we decided to go to swim, so we drove to the cape of Borzovka. Vladimir told the children and the driver, "Do not rush into the water. First cool off, then go to swim." Later he added to Ivan, "And you go dive into the water and come right back to the automobile. We will be going on soon."

They went to swim and I stayed behind. While I was conversing with the people, suddenly Larisa came running and shouting, "Our driver perished!" "How did he perish?" I asked. "Look!" she said. As I looked I saw Vladimir was still swimming, looking for Ivan, and from the shore people were shouting and showing him where Ivan plunged into the water. Later those who were at the seashore were telling that Moiseyev came to the surface, shouted something, and went down again.

Ten minutes went by. Vladimir was still looking for Moiseyev. Then suddenly a wave brought his body up to the surface. His body was immediately picked up by the people and given artificial respiration. They sent me to get an ambulance. Not far away was either a boarding school or a holiday house. I called the ambulance. In the meantime a doctor from that place came to the seashore.

The doctor began to give him artificial respiration. Then he said, "Get me some alcohol." Where can one get alcohol? We went to the tents at the seashore; tourists lived in the tents. They had some alcohol.

Somebody was shouting at the doctor, "Whatever you need, tell us and we will find it. If we only could save the young man's life." But the massage with alcohol did not help. The doctor said, "We need to apply mustard plaster." Mustard was found in the tents.

The ambulance arrived. They gave an injection to Moiseyev. Shortly after another ambulance arrived. They gave another injection and gave him artificial respiration.

For three hours they worked on Ivan, trying to bring him back to life; unfortunately, all efforts seemed to be in vain. About fifty people gathered around Ivan's body, and they all were weeping bitterly at the death of the young soldier.

Now, all of a sudden I find out that there are some slanderers who took advantage of such deep grief for their provoking purposes. The marks which were left in effort to save Moiseyev's life were used as a proof of torture. One must be unscrupulously cynical to do such a thing! I know where the slander came from. I was still there when the relatives came to take Ivan's body. One of them just looked at the deceased, and without even giving tribute of grief began to affirm, "I know they killed him, they tortured him to death." It seemed to me that he already came with a prepared version and was looking

202

for every possible way to confirm it. How can the leaders of the Evangelical Christian/Baptist church talk about sanctity and love toward your neighbor when they themselves lack the simple human conscience! To what kind of high ideals of faith can they call their coreligionists?

There were fifty of us who witnessed Ivan Moiseyev's death. And if people who declare Ivan their brother speculate on his death, if they sell conscience for thirty imported silver coins, then we will not permit them to take advantage of the misfortune of others; we will not permit them to hide their black souls behind the filthy slander.

L.A. Martinenko,
inhabitant of the city of Stavropola.

Condolences to the Moiseyevs from all parts of the USSR (reprinted in CPR Bulletin No. 11)

БЮЛЛЕТЕНЬ

СОВЕТА РОДСТВЕННИКОВ УЗНИКОВ
ЕВАНГЕЛЬСКИХ ХРИСТИАН-БАПТИСТОВ В СССР

"...Помните узников, как бы и вы с ними были в узах, и страждущих..."
Евр. 13,13.

11

г. Москва 1973 г.

The cover of the 60-page handwritten bulletin

Letters from soldiers

FROM: *Four soldiers in the Red army: Leysha, Alexis, Valerik, and Meesha in the city of Bobruisk.*

We are maintaining a prayer watch beginning with a minute's silence in honor of the martyr death of our dear friend and soldier, Vanya. Although we have never seen him, we have been washed and made to be brothers by the blood of Christ for which we give Him eternal thanks.

Last August we learned of the martyr death of our brother Vanya, and like no one else we have felt the sorrow because we are in the same circumstances. We are wearing the same kind of uniform, we are living among the same kind of people, and we are anticipating returning to our beloved fathers and mothers, which for him never came to pass. The heart becomes heavy when one looks at packed suitcases which we will be able to pick up with our hands in a few days and will be able to say "Hello, mama"—and he did not have this joy. However, he had a better meeting, the meeting with his Lord.

We would like, if possible, to comfort you, stand together with you, and take upon ourselves your sorrow. We know that your loss is beyond your strength to bear. Many have attempted to comfort you. However we believe that the angel of Vanya up to this day has not left you. He is with you day and night to comfort you. He will wipe your tears. Yes, every tear he will carry up into heaven and when you will meet your God at His throne where you will greet His Son, the twelve apostles, the Church, and the angels, God will press you to His bosom and will wipe your tears forever. This will take place very soon.

The enemy tried to destroy the soul of Vanya, hoping that he would deny his faith. But God came to the rescue of his soul when the enemy in merciless wrath threw himself upon his flesh and took away his breathing. The enemy thought he would close Vanya's mouth, but he did not reckon that by this act he will open thousands of mouths. Yes, the mouth of one courageous soldier was closed. But our mouths are not closed. We are continuing to carry the news of salvation to all who are perishing. We are telling everybody how God revealed His power in miracles. How unmercifully Vanya was beaten; about that we can not be silent. We have the same spirit of faith according as it is written, "I believed and therefore have I spoken." We also believe and therefore speak. Many listen to us with much longing, and now when we give them the bulletin they are even more interested. They take it home with them and show it and witness to their friends. We believe that many mouths will be opened. We do not say anything to the officers, but the soldiers who read the account and see the photograph are telling other soldiers about the power of God and the faithfulness of His children. If the enemy closes our mouths, then others will be raised up. Let them punish us, deprive us of everything on this earth. But they will not be able to take the freedom of Christ out of our hearts.

Almost every evening we go out into the little garden for prayer, where we receive much from the Lord and see His hand with us. When we heard about the heroic labor and death of our friend and brother Vanya, his martyr death, we strengthened our knees even more. The prayer watch which was Vanya's responsibility is not forsaken. God has put the flame into our hearts, and we with the help of God will diligently carry the watch of prayer in the army. Let the enemy know it; the work of God is standing on a firm and eternal foundation. And he will never break our determination. We are maintaining a prayer watch. We, the soldiers in the evening, go out to the place of prayer, and with a minute's silence honor the memory of the martyr death of our dear friend and soldier Vanya, who gave his life for Christ. We are keeping the sorrow in our hearts. It hurts that the enemy has the power to take the life of God's faithful children.

We of course are not allowed to pray, to get together; our New Testaments have been taken away from us in the hope of reeducation, but by this they are igniting the flame even more.

We are not left alone. We have much bread.

Dear Moiseyev family, don't be discouraged. God has done a great work in the salvation of souls through your dear son and our brother and friend, our peer Vanya. He moved forward; he did not confer with flesh and blood. Jesus gave him the order and gave him a banner which he had to carry through fire and storm. Vanya fulfilled the order and reported about its fulfillment, and now there awaits him eternal glory and reward from the loving Father. God will undoubtedly give you a reward, dear father and mother. You reared your son in the Spirit and in truth. You ignited in him the longing of communion with God.

Soon the eternity you long for will be exchanged
for your pain on life's way,

And with great love to you who have suffered much
angels will give the best crown in that day.

FROM: *A discharged soldier, Kolia, in the city of Kirovsk.*

Before I came into the army, I knew little about Christ. But in the army I heard nothing about Him. Since being discharged from the army I have heard much about Christ, but I didn't want to believe and didn't want to accept Him. But Christ Himself called me, and I am very grateful to my Savior Christ that He did not leave me in a perishing condition.

After my service in the army, I was an active *Komsomoltzem* [a member of the Young Communist League]. I was an active participant in sport and was a Komsomol organizer where I worked. I had plans to enroll in an institute, but when the Lord called me to Himself and to serve Him I put my Komsomol card down and refused to participate in sport. After that, the door into the institute was closed for me. But I am grateful to my Savior Jesus Christ for His love to me so that I am now saved through the blood of Jesus Christ. I have eternal life. Praise and honor to our Savior Christ.

Yes, our dear brother in Christ Vanya Moiseyev left an example for us how we should live and fight or battle and die. Our dear brother Ivan will be in our hearts eternally. He suffered much torture, but he was faithful to Christ to the end. He left us an example of how to strive for the crown of Christ.

I am twenty-three years old, and up to this year I was in the world. My mother is a believer. I have no father. She told me often about Christ, but I did not accept her teaching because I loved the world and its works in which I was more interested than in Christ. My mother could not persuade me to leave the world and to serve Christ. She prayed to Christ for us, and He heard her. One night I had a revelation. I saw Christ, who called me to Himself and to His service. After a short time, the Lord appeared to me again in a dream. Now I am a servant of Christ, and I thank Him for everything, that He did not leave me in this sinful world. Praise be to Christ for His love to all of us.

FROM: *Two soldiers, Victor and Alexis, in the city of Kirovobad.*

Greetings from soldiers unknown to you. Please excuse us for invading your life, but by chance we heard the history of your son's last days of life. This history touched us and troubled us, and we decided to write you a letter to ask you to give us the details. Of course if it is possible, would you describe his life to us just a little bit?

Letters from believers

FROM: *A young girl, Luba, in the Rovno region.*

I am two years younger than Vanya. I am also a member of the church of Christ. I believe the heroic deed of Vanya will inspire and strengthen all who will know about him both young and old. Through Vanya many will come and worship God. I have no papa. That is, he does not live with us. I have only my dear mother. But I am grateful to the Lord that she is a believer. When I was little she prayed for me and she was able to put into my heart this holy charge. The Lord has called me to follow Him. I thank Him and I rejoice that He is dearer to me than all and everything. Looking at the photograph and reading about him [Vanya], I will always be inspired to faithfulness and to willingness to do everything for Christ. Because of perishing people our way is cruel, the road is difficult, and there is much work here. And we are all needed without exception. Forward with haste and all together, brothers.

FROM: *A schoolgirl, Maria, in the Altai Novo'Blagoveshchenski district.*

I am sixteen. I am a member of the church. I was baptized in water one year later than Vanya Moiseyev. Having received word that he died very mysteriously, we are in deep sorrow and are supporting you in our prayer. Everything that happens is in God's will.

FROM: *A man, Ivan, in the city of Niesvezh, BSSR.*

Ivan Vasilievich was faced with a great trial, and with the help of God he endured it. Praise God for this feat. He became like the following: Stephen, John Hus, Shadrach, Meshach, and Abed-nego, Daniel, Jeremiah, and many others. He accomplished everything and is now awaiting the crown of righteousness—II Timothy 4:6-8.

FROM: *A young man, Milail, in the village of Kokoryavka, Braynsk region.*

I learned about the martyrdom of Vanya from the bulletin. Oh, what a way he had to Christ! The reason for my letter is that I want to be like Ivan Moiseyev.

FROM: *A schoolgirl, Galya, in the Lvov region.*

In our city there is a small, unregistered assembly of about twenty members. One of our brothers has been sentenced to three years of imprisonment, but we are still struggling. We have a good defender—Christ. We are despised in school. I am the oldest of three girls. In 1971 my girlfriend Lucia used to wear a red necktie,* but she's from a family of believers and stopped wearing it.

I went with her to a [Christian] fellowship of young people, and our teachers learned about this and started to oppress me. Many times they interrogated me. Now they tell me, "You are walking in darkness. You don't go to the movies or to the theaters and you are dragging your girlfriend the same way." One day in the presence of all the students in the class I was interrogated for a whole class period, but this did not grieve me. On the contrary, I was quite happy, and I prayed, because with Christ I was defeating the enemy. Brothers and sisters, do not think that I am bragging. No, dear friends, I am simply sharing about the little unnoticed struggle that I have with the enemy.

People of Christ, dare and go forward.
Break down the strongholds of unbelief.
Call, awaken to the salvation of the people.
Proclaim the victory of Jesus.

---

*The red kerchief is worn by all Young Pioneers.

FROM: *A man, Pavel, in the city of Pinsk.*

Recently my wife and I visited the city of Riga and there we happened to learn the name of God's hero of the twentieth century, the courageous Christian, Vanya Moiseyev. The group in Riga wept and admired his firmness. Praise the Lord for such a hero Christian. There are many believers in our city, especially young people.

FROM: *A woman, Valentina, in the city of Leningrad.*

The great God, the Creator of the universe, has made you to be the torchbearers in your village and also in all of the earth. We praise Him that His power is made perfect in weakness through those who are nothing in this world, the most insignificant ones in the world, that the mighty ones of this world may be put to shame. Roma tried to commit our address to memory and destroyed all of the envelopes. Be wise.

> Like a ladder before me my faith ascends;
> Arise, oh, my timid soul, rise up, rise up.
> Give faith! A thankful heart on You depends
> Oh, Thou Savior I pray.
>
> By faith bathed in a beautiful light
> I gaze up at Thee, O living Head,
> I long for swift answers to prayer in my sight
> More faith in my heart.
>
> Turn stones into bread before unfeeling men,
> Let me move mountains and praise You again.

FROM: *A woman, Vera, in the city of Kaisk, Siberia.*

We live in faraway Siberia. How true that there are still those resisting. Like the Word says, "You have not resisted to the point of shedding blood" Hebrews 12:4.

FROM: *A schoolgirl, Maria, in the Altiy region.*

I was born in 1956; in August I will be seventeen years old. And I am already a member of a church. I repented of my sins in 1971, the third of January in the morning at ten-forty-five. I was baptized in 1971 on the eighteenth of July in the morning.

Mother, I am afraid; no God I know;
Please tell me an eternal way to go.
You taught me how to live, each day by day,
But I am dying and you don't know what to say.

In our land we honor mothers high
The very word *mother* exalted to the sky
But only the mother with God in her heart
Can teach her child how this life to part.

FROM: *A woman, Natasha, in the city of Slavianogorsk.*

Hundreds of those persecuted will bear much fruit
Adding strength without measure, new champions recruit.

Hebrews 10:35. There are many roads we have to travel where the winds are contrary. We will be tired and will be counting the remaining miles. Many daily sorrows we have to experience in this world. It may be that we have to be deprived of our children, of our jobs and our homes: innocent, but proclaimed guilty and slandered by a brother. We may be called to walk in deep darkness and to live in the atmosphere of godlessness and blasphemy. But still it pays to believe. We will stand before Christ at the judgment.

FROM: *A woman, Masha, in rural Kirov.*

I live way back in the country and therefore only recently did I learn about the heroic feat of our brother Vanya. I hope and believe that his martyrdom will bring a hundredfold harvest and will serve to revive the sleeping Christians to a new life, and that many, many young people will come to Christ in repentance, and the ranks of Christian youth will be increased. I believe in God the Almighty. He is powerful to do this even here in our little town where only two other sisters and I are believers.

FROM: *A grandfather in the city of Kiev.*

I am seventy-four years of age. Having read your letter in our home together with my family, I share with and sympathize with your earthly sorrow. But I am rejoicing that in this manner we can have fellowship with you. I am your brother in Christ and a participant in the experiences and sorrows of tortures and in trials. I was apart from my family eleven years in Kolima, a place of exile. Now I am seventy-four years old. From my youth I have dedicated my life to the Lord. I have three sons, and they are all serving the Lord. We praise Him for his call. I am an invalid. From the exile I came back with one arm, but alive. Accept my greetings.

FROM: *A woman, Polina, in the Tula region.*

I very deeply share your sorrow and your tears.

In heaven our tears will become purest gold;
The death of a martyr will be turned into gain.
How poor are those men whose lives do not hold
Earthly sorrow and suffering and pain.

They are not pulled by God's heavenly light
They cannot desire God's rest and delight.

Here in front of me is a photograph of our dear friend Vanya with his signature. Faithful servant of God—yes, truly he was a hero of faith. In the full meaning of this word, he loved Christ and he wholly gave his useful heart to Christ.

FROM: *A young woman, Nadia, in Kiev.*

When I read in the bulletin the short biography of Vanya, the miracles that happened to him, and about his untimely death, I was shocked. I admire his firmness, the power of his love toward Christ, his self-sacrifice, his willingness to sacrifice his life in order that he may prove that there is a God and that He is almighty and omnipotent. Vanya wished only the best to the people around him. He used all his power to bring them to repentance. He preached Christ, the crucified. He is all love and purity, and Vanya wanted that others would be like him before the Lord. Alas, they did not accept and did not understand him. Foolish, cruel murderers. They crucified Vanya just like his beloved Jesus Christ was crucified. *Dearest Vanya, how cruelly you suffered; at the same time you are so fortunate.*

Now he is living somewhere in the heavenly kingdom, far from this sinful world. Up there it rains only peace and love. I, too, want to be like Vanya, and if necessary to die like he did, remaining faithful to Jesus. Right now I am asking the Lord that he would teach me to pray and to serve him as Vanya served him—Vanya, my brother in Christ.

FROM: *A young girl, Luba, in the city of Ferganafrom.*

A seed is sown,
It is watered with blood,
God's people know
Much fruit will come.

There are ten in our family. Vanya has become for us young people the symbol of faith, hope, and love. We have understood that the spring of our life, our youth, we must give wholly to the service of the Lord, even if the Lord will take it forever. Without wavering, we must agree to do what Vanya has done. We have our own dear bulletin about Vanya with his photograph and have it placed in a prominent place. When we meet with difficulties, then, always looking at the portrait of Vanya, we are comforted. He looks at us with that penetrating look as if he were asking, "Friend, are you ready to walk this earthly way like I walked?" And then one falls on his knees and answers, "Oh, Lord, give me this kind of faith, that I too could imitate him like he imitated Thee."

FROM: *A woman, Maria, in the village of Pokrovka, Kirgis SSR.*

I am deeply persuaded in the sincerity of the write-up. I was so shook up by this death and by the cruelty of the Soviet people over God's people that all the time I see it before me; even at night I can not sleep because of all that has happened. I was shocked by his faithfulness to God. The bulletin is going from hand to hand. One such bulletin, to our great regret, has been taken by the police.

FROM: *A mother, Evdokia, in the city of Bobrinetz.*

The word of the suffering of your beloved son shook up many churches of Christ here. My children and I could not sleep because of the sorrow that was drilling in our hearts as if he were our own son. Our father was imprisoned twice and had to leave me alone—the first time for one year, and the second time for five years with strict regimen—a five-year exile. How unpleasant it is to hear that in our time, our government has carried out this terrible mission. To think that there were cruel executioners who were not afraid to take the life and flower from that young branch, when they did not give it to him.

FROM: *A woman, Evrosinia, in the Donetz region.*

My Christian love for you and for your son who suffered so much for Jesus Christ impells us to write to you. Reading the whole story, we also saw a photo of Vanya. We live in a large

215

village, but the believers are few—only five persons. We go to our gospel meeting in a city twelve miles from here. Come over here. Good-by.

FROM: *An older woman, Tatyana, in the city of Achinsk, Krosnotar region.*

I share your sorrow for your Vanya. I read and reread, weep and pray, and at the same time I rejoice for his faithfulness and for the beautiful bouquet of his youth which he gave to the Lord as a gift. I gave him the autumn of my life, and the stream of His water of grace is only up to my ankle. It has been only two years since I have been baptized.

FROM: *A woman, Galina, in the Lvov region.*

I sat down to read about Vanya, and I was enveloped with a feeling of joy for Vanya that he did not bow before the enemy and that the enemy did not see him broken, but he saw him faithful to God to the end. I no longer wept. No, I sang. I sang the hymn of youth. Greetings to you, Christ's blooming tribe, also to all the corners of this unhappy earth and our wonderful land. I rejoiced, and I rejoice that we have such good exemplary brothers and sisters to whom a golden crown belongs.

FROM: *A schoolgirl, Galina, in the city of Brody.*

Everything is fine here. The Lord is with us and He is directing us. Our weather is very strange. In the morning it freezes. At twelve o'clock the sun shines and at six o'clock it rains. But however, we can work for the Lord in all kinds of weather.

I have started a thick notebook where I am writing good wishes and greetings. On the first page I have a flower. On the second and third pages are poems of Vanya Moiseyev which I copied from the bulletin. And all this I have decorated with flowers. I treasure this notebook very much. As a sign of our Christian greeting, please accept this poem.

Be from your youth a soldier of Christ,
Be from your youth a champion for right.
As the soldier you are, slash with your sword
And vanquish sin's night.

FROM: *A man, Pavel, in the city of Kislovodsk.*

God performs miracles in our days with the same power as in the past. Dear friends, this incident has circled the whole country and it is impelling us to action and prayer. The time will come when we will see Vanya enjoy praising God. Will you be there? Yes, he is there already.

FROM: *A woman, Luba, in the city of Azh'Abad.*

"Blessed are you when men revile you, and persecute you, and say all kinds of evil against you falsely, on account of Me" (Matthew 5:11). And Matthew 5:4—"Blessed are those who mourn, for they shall be comforted." The Lord be with you; fear not.

Forward, forward in God's name,
Forward, forward for the perishing's sake
His way is not heeded
We are all needed
Every one.

Forward with haste, together, brothers.

FROM: *Brothers in the United States.*

Our dear ones, we love you. We weep with you, but we are happy that your son was faithful. You will see him in heaven. We will always pray for you.

Letters from unbelievers

FROM: *A man, Romaniukel, in the city of Bratsk.*

I want to know if Vasiliy Trofimovich Moiseyev lives here. Did you have a son, Ivan? Do you actually believe in God? To what denomination do you belong?

FROM: *A young woman, Rita, in the city of Altai.*

With much emotion I read about your son in the bulletin and I had to write a letter. At the present time I am an unbeliever, but I want very much to be like Vanya. I cannot even think without emotion about his terrible death. I want very much to be like him. He loved Jesus Christ very much. Yes, he loved Him more than anybody. But how can I attain this? How remarkable. He is a hero for me and he will be my example. Excuse me if something I have written isn't just right. I could not refrain from writing.

FROM: *A young man, Leonid Alexandrovich, in the city of Brest.*

I learned about your sorrow and I was very disturbed about what has happened to your son, Ivan. Up to this moment I did not even imagine that something like that could take place here. My blood boils when I think of the behavior of your son Semyon, a brother of Vanya. I have a sister who is a believer, but if anything happened to her like what happened to your Vanya, I would not have behaved like Semyon. Please tell him that. Excuse this very short letter. Good-by.

FROM: *A man, V. I. Sergeichuk, in the Rovno region.*

To the esteemed Moiseyev family: hello. Excuse this stranger who will bother you. I have met strangers who told me very much about your son Vanya. For my own information I decided to write to you and to find out where your son

Vanya is and how is getting along. Awaiting your reply.
Good-by.

FROM: *A young girl, Maria, in the village of Galina, in Volia.*

Excuse me for troubling your heart with my letter. I am a resident of the village of Galina, Volia, a simple farm worker. In our village there are many believers, and I had the opportunity to read in the bulletin about the martyrdom of your son. Of course, I am an unbeliever, but having seen all this, I cannot remain silent. May the Lord be with you.

A reply

FROM: *Vanya's parents to a group of atheists in the city of Ryazan.*

Among the multitude of letters of condolence which we received after the martyrdom of our son, Ivan, for faith in God, we read yours.

For your sympathy we thank you. Our son died from the torture of fanatical atheists who have the authority and the sword. We read the bulletin #9 of the Council of ECB Prisoners' Relatives in the USSR. We confirm that everything that was written in the bulletin about our son is true. We are keeping his last letters, the copies of which were printed in the bulletin. We are saving the recording tape on which are recorded Vanya's narratives about the horrors he experienced even before his death as a martyr. For greater clarity about conditions of believers in our country, we advise that you read all of the foregoing bulletins of the Council of Prisoners' Relatives. With questions about additional evidence of the martyrdom you may turn to the judicial medical experts, to the main procurator of the armed forces, and to Dr. Potapov in the city of Kerch, who performed the autopsy on Vanya's body.

We beg you in the name of Jesus, against whom you have been fighting, and perhaps are still fighting—be reconciled to God.

The Moiseyevs

December 1972

Publisher's Note

Persons wishing to obtain more information on Christianity in the Soviet Union may contact one of the following agencies:

Amnesty International
53 Theobald's Road
London WCIX 8SP
Great Britain

Jesus to the Communist World, Inc.
P. O. Box 11
Glendale, CA 91209

Center for the Study of Religion and Communism
  (U.S. Branch)
P.O. Box 1122
Wheaton, IL 60187

Christian Mission Publishers
3194 Dundas Street W.
Toronto, Ontario
Canada

Eastern European Bible Mission
P. O. Box 73
Walnut Creek, CA 94596

Eastern European Mission
232 N. Lake Ave.
Pasadena, Calif. 91101

Open Doors with Brother Andrew
P.O. Box 2020
Orange, Calif. 92669

Russia for Christ
P.O. Box 30000
Santa Barbara, Calif. 93105

Slavic Gospel Association
P. O. Box 1122
Wheaton, IL 60187

Slavic Missionary Society
P.O. Box 307
South River, N.J. 08882